SPORTS OFFICIATING
A Legal Guide

DEDICATION

To the officials of New Jersey

SPORTS OFFICIATING
A Legal Guide

Alan S. Goldberger, J. D.

LEISURE PRESS

NEW YORK

A publication of
Leisure Press
P.O. Box 3, West Point, N.Y. 10996
Copyright © 1984 Leisure Press
All rights reserved. Printed in the U.S.A.

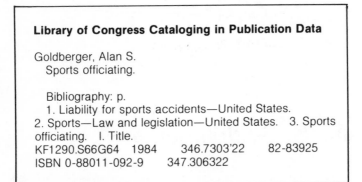

Library of Congress Cataloging in Publication Data

Goldberger, Alan S.
  Sports officiating.

  Bibliography: p.
  1. Liability for sports accidents—United States.
  2. Sports—Law and legislation—United States.   3. Sports
  officiating.   I. Title.
  KF1290.S66G64   1984   346.7303'22   82-83925
  ISBN 0-88011-092-9   347.306322

Front cover photo: Cal Photo

CONTENTS

ACKNOWLEDGMENTS

In 15 years of officiating, a fellow makes a lot of friends and, to be sure, a comparable number of "acquaintances." All of them have, in some way, contributed to this book.

Beyond that, there are many individuals who actively participated in the fine tuning of what you are about to read, and generously gave of their time and knowledge.

Very special thanks go to my three fiercest critics, all outstanding young attorneys who were instrumental in making this book a reality. Douglas M. Lehman, of Pavia & Harcourt of the New York bar; the Honorable Fred J. Levin, Judge of the Cherry Hill, New Jersey Municipal Court; and Lorre Sylvan Smith, of the New Jersey bar, spent long hours gnawing on the manuscript until they were sure I had said what I wanted to say.

For their efforts, as well as the untiring diligence of my typist and editor extraordinare, Miriam Goldberger, I am grateful beyond words.

Nor could this book have been completed without the invaluable assistance of my two good friends, Professor Harry W. Nowick, Head Coach of Soccer at Essex County College, and Richard Matarante, secretary of the New Jersey Wrestling Officials' Association. Harry's long and illustrious officiating career has made him a legend in his own time. Dick, one of New Jersey's premier wrestling officials, has successfully officiated and coached baseball and football for many years on the high school level.

Special thanks also go to Jeffereson D. Bates, Don Gasaway, Esq., Megan O'Neill, Esq., Jim Rosati, veteran football official and secretary of the New Jersey Football Official's Association, North Jersey Chapter; to my "ace" photographer, Robert Bruckner; and to Theresa O'Connell, Caaron Willinger, and Marc Bruckner of my office.

And, last but certainly not least, my hearfelt thanks goes to my publisher, Dr. Jim Peterson and his fine staff at Leisure Press, Inc.

FOREWORD

In the complex and litigious 1980s our American legal system may appear to be incomprehensible to the non-professional, in view of the seemingly endless procession of unfamiliar language, obscure definitions and intractable procedures. All of us daily encounter transactions both in our personal and business affairs which appear simple yet may have widespread legal ramifications.

Certainly, the legal system has had a strong impact in the contemporary world of sports and athletic competition, both amateur and professional. Officials must act as judge in the heat of athletic competition without the benefit of deliberation. Whether it's a game of sandlot baseball or a multi-million dollar World Series, the outcome may be determined by an individual official's judgment, a decision often forgotten by evening or debated for decades to come. All of us are familiar with the celebrated legal disputes in professional athletics, but we are frequently unaware of the impact of the legal system on less publicized everyday sporting events. The official is clearly an affected participant.

An official needs a working familiarity with those areas of the law pertaining to his avocation. In this book, you'll find a straight and candid discussion of frequently asked questions involving the legal aspects of officiating, ranging from liability for players' injuries to the role of officials' association. This book is a complete source of information on the important legal concerns of every official.

Alan Goldberger is eminently qualified as the author of this unique book for today's knowledgeable sports official. In my many years as Alan's personal friend and professional colleague, I have come to be both an admirer and unabashed fan. In addition to his extensive experience as a baseball, basketball and football official, Alan currently serves as legal adviser to numerous officials' associations and groups. He has combined over 16 years of active officiating with his expertise as an accomplished practicing attorney, enabling him to evaluate the need of today's sports official from each critical perspective. Hence this book.

Sports Officiating: A Legal Guide is, quite simply, the first and only handbook which provides the sports official with clear, concise, sound guidance on legal principles which relate to the task of officiating.

—Fred Jay Levin
Cherry Hill, New Jersey
Municipal Court Judge

1

INTRODUCTION:
WHY THIS BOOK WAS WRITTEN

We "zebras" are in danger of becoming extinct, you know.

People have been calling officials "zebras" probably since the first day one of us donned the black and white striped jersey. Along the way, of course, we've been called other things, too. But then, what leads one to think that the two-legged "zebra" is headed for the list of endangered species?

It seems to me that two trends have developed in late 20th century America which have combined to make survival for game officials a greater challenge than ever before.

In the past few years, much has been written about the general decline in respect for authority of any kind. This trend spans society from young to old—cutting across all socioeconomic and geographical distinctions: people are no longer content to hear "yes" or "no"—there is always the question "Why?"

Increasingly, the question "Why?" is being asked and answered in court. The so-called litigation explosion is characterized by a many-fold increase in the number of lawsuits filed, coupled with a wide expansion in the type and character of matters that are now being decided by judges and juries.

As officials, we are often threatened and sometimes attacked, both verbally and physically. The emphasis placed upon "winning" results is making challenging the referee's decision more fashionable than ever. Tune in to any televised game and see for yourself.

How many times has the "star" who happened to commit his fifth foul in front of you blamed you for his mistake? How many times has—in the eyes of the players and fans—your "bad call" cost the team a victory? Do you really think any athlete will hesitate to name you in a lawsuit if he is injured during a game you are working? I don't.

Once in court, we can reasonably expect to have the same friends supporting us that we have on the field or court, i.e., our officiating partners. More unfortunately, in some situations, we should anticipate that we cannot even have the support of our colleagues from other sports, from other associations, or even from games other than the game involved in the incident in which we seek to assert our rights or defend our actions.

Therefore, every official should be aware of the legal ramifications of his actions, his relationship to his fellow officials, and to the athletes for whom he toils—and have a healthy respect for the concept that the legal rights of all officials must be asserted—or the "zebra" may indeed someday become extinct: If the avocation becomes so unattractive in the wake of assaults, public sharp-shooting by biased and uninformed media commentators, and the refusal of administrators to adequately compensate officials and provide a decent and safe working environment, fewer men and women will undertake what is often a thankless task.

In this book, I will attempt to analyze some of the more common occurrences which can affect you as an official in terms of a lawsuit being brought against you. Further, if you are injured, abused, or otherwise mistreated, I will tell you what your rights are, how to assert them, what to do and what not to do. One of the most honored concepts for officiating any sport is that of preventive officiating. We can carry this concept one step further and exercise preventive officiating for ourselves, as well as for the athletes we serve. For every time an official is abused and does nothing, in a very real sense, we are all hurt.

That being said, please understand that I certainly don't intend to presume to tell any official how to officiate, or to prescribe a certain course of conduct as being the "correct" way. I certainly do not presume to tell an official what is "right" and what is "wrong" with respect to his actions on and off the field and court.

I do, however, suggest to you that the methods of dealing with situations as outlined in this book will, if employed in a manner consistent with common sense, greatly minimize your legal exposure as an official. It's my further hope that knowing how to recognize the situations in which you may need to call upon the legal system to assert your rights will make life easier for you and for all other officials.

The suggestions contained in this book are designed to keep you out of legal trouble, and to enable you to effectively use the legal system and your lawyer to assert your legal rights when necessary.

I will not attempt to tell you that it is "right" or "wrong" to take or refrain from taking a given course of action. Nor are the observations in these pages intended to be a be all and end all of officiating ethics or morals.

Finally, let me tell you what this book is not. This book is not an officiating manual. My hope is that it will make you, having read and digested the material, a better official. For it is my firm belief, after many years as an official and a practicing attorney, that utilizing the techniques contained in this book, *you will in fact be a better official.*

And, most importantly, you will be doing your job, the way you are supposed to do it, in the fashion for which you were contracted to do it, and you will be acting as an official should act. Thus, you will have the respect of the athletes, the coaches, your fellow officials, and, most importantly, yourself.

2

BEFORE THE GAME

Sometimes the strangest things happen long before the referee's whistle to start the game. And if you're not ready for everything and anything by the time you set your bag down on the dressing room bench, you're in trouble!

A few years back, on a beautiful Thanksgiving morning, my partners and I (I was the field judge) were preparing to assume our pre-game duties. Our referee and umpire had set out to visit both teams' locker rooms, and the linesman and I set out for the field to begin our inspections, etc. Upon arrival at the playing field, the linesman and I proceeded to head for the end zone, noting the sideline markings and looking for any hazards or difficulties that might affect the game. When we got to the first end zone, we noticed that the pylons marking the intersection of the goal line and sideline were made of hard, Styrofoam-type material.This is of course illegal under the National Federation Football Code in that pylons must be of soft, flexible material. The reason for this is obvious: an unyielding pylon, being a 4″ square and 18″ high cylinder, can act as a spear or weapon puncturing whatever part of the unfortunate player's torso that happens to land on it. The legal pylons are made of collapsible foam rubber which bends on contact and, in fact, can be twisted like a pretzel. Thus, no matter which way someone falls or is tackled onto it, or lands on it, it can't do any damage.

Back to business:

Anyway, we figured maybe this was a bad one and went on to the next. Sure enough, the pylon at the intersection of the endline and the sideline was made of the same substance. We found the same situation in the other end zone.

Our choice was clear; play the game with unsafe equipment and subject ourselves to all of the unpleasant consequences that may follow, or play the game without pylons. Needless to say, we opted for the latter alternative. Simple enough? Not quite. We approached the grounds keepers, advising them of the pylons and requesting they remove them. They seemed rather upset at this request, and, in fact, walked away muttering that they would do no such thing. The next thing we know, the athletic director appears on the field and begins to rant and rave that the game would be played with the pylons in place and that better officials than we had permitted their use. This responsible administrator of athletic programs for young men and women further indicated that he would draw "officials" from the stands to officiate the game if we didn't want to work.

Admidst the tirade, we informed the athletic director that the game would be played *without* the illegal pylons or not at all. When it became clear to him that our position was non-negotiable, he removed the pylons with great fanfare. What caused this particularly bizarre behavior on the part of the athletic director remains a mystery. But, the point is, you must have what it takes to "stick to your guns" and protect yourself from senseless exposure to legal liability—and sometimes at a high cost in terms of pre-game tranquility.

So, when you go out to referee, if you think you have a lot of supporters hanging around the bleachers or on the sidelines, I've got news for you! You're mistaken. If there is only one item of importance that you pick up from this book, I want it to be this; when you go out to officiate, your fellow official(s) is(are) your only friend(s). All veteran officials know this. Many young officials learn the hard way. Illustrations aplenty are found in these pages. For now, suffice it to say that there are precious few persons present at any athletic event who entertain the same thoughts about the competition that day that you do.

What are you interested in? You are interested in conducting the game in accordance with the rules in a fashion so the team that plays better on that particular day will win. You are interested in seeing that no one gets hurt, and that both teams have an equal chance to win. You don't care which one. You don't care which player strikes out or fouls out. You don't care if it's a no-hitter or if one of the teams can't advance the ball beyond its own 20-yard line.

Yet you must be at your best every play. You must be consistently alert, but not overbearing. You often are expected to supervise an area as large, as they say, as a football field—and you have to have the ability to control fast moving and powerful young men and women who are programmed to deceive their opponents, and sometimes to deceive you.

Richard Clegg and William A. Thompson, in their excellent book, *Modern Sports Officiating: A Practical Guide* (William C. Brown Company, Dubuque, Iowa, 1974, 1979), list what they consider to be four essential ingredients of a successful official:

- Intelligent rule book enforcement. Clegg & Thompson cite the "Tower philosophy" for the proposition that good jugment is a necessary adjunct to intelligent rule enforcement. Oldtimers will remember the "Tower philosophy" attributable to the late Oswald Tower as a hall mark of intelligent officiating. Briefly stated, the "Tower philosophy" has as its cornerstone the ability and judgment to distinguish between those infractions which place an opponent at a disadvantage and those technical infractions which have no bearing on the competition.

- Absolute integrity. Clegg & Thompson relate this not only to being influenced by extraneous factors such as score, time remaining, crowd reaction, but also to the area of accepting assignments and general conduct.

- Establishment of sound human relations. This is broken down into relationships with fellow officials, players, coaches and spectators.

- A successful official must show "primary concern for the individual athlete." In this section, it is urged that a successful official is concerned with preventing injuries, encouraging sportsmanship, improving player performance through correct rulings, not discouraging questions on the rules, and attempting to keep players in the game rather than disqualifying them while having the fortitude to disqualify a player when necessary.

In summarizing these qualities, Clegg & Thompson conclude:

The official who is able and willing to use protection of the players as a guide will be amazed at its effectiveness, especially in making difficult decisions.

Everybody wants to see his or her team win. That's the "fun" of sport! Therefore, when one of your decisions or non-decisions goes the way of one team, its personnel and supporters think that they are getting simply what they deserve—justice, no more; no less. Are you likely to be applauded? I think not.

On the other hand, the opponents of the team in whose favor your call goes may well take issue with what you have done. Even if you are absolutely right, they may take issue with you with what you have called because:

- of the way you have called it;
- of the way they have seen it; or
- they think they will "set you up" for the next call.

Moreover, on the part of the players, this displeasure with your decision often serves as a suitable alibi for the player's own short-comings, errors of judgment or failure to be able to make the requisite maneuver.

The player who is called out on a 3-2 pitch with a bat on his shoulder will use his arguing with the home-plate umpire over the call to inform not only the spectators but his teammates, the other team, and a grimacing manager that it wasn't his fault that he struck out, but rather the plate umpire's.

The same coach who slaps you on the back and tells you what a great game you worked tonight, may not hesitate to broadcast your incompetence to the local newspaper or television station if he feels you took something away from him in a subsequent game.

Going hand in hand with the concept of acknowledging who your friends are and who your friends aren't when you go to officiate is the concept of *keeping your objectives in mind*. What does this mean? When Woody Allen said, "Showing up is 80 percent of life," he clearly was not referring to officials. You've got to do more.

Although all of us are "crazy" about sports or we wouldn't be offi-ciating, we cannot assume or propose to wear more than one hat when we are engaged to referee or umpire athletic competition. When you appear in a gymnasium, whether it be a tiny parish house with linoleum floors or Pauley Pavillion, and you are the official; that's your only purpose. Your objective is to referee the game. Not to be a fan, cheerleader, scout, entrepreneur or vendor of uniforms or pos-ters. You're just a referee. Seek no other connections or relation-ships. People will misinterpret what you are doing if you're trying to sell something related to your business.

If you're a salesman of uniforms, don't attempt to make a sales call on the athletic director prior to officiating at that school. If you're promoting a special event at the school where you teach, don't bring posters and ask the faculty member in charge where you should put them up. In short, don't ingratiate yourself. Don't do anything that will lead anyone to accuse you of double-dealing with respect to any of the institutions or persons for whom you will be working as an active official.

The reason for this is simple: You must be indebted to no one and no one must be indebted to you. If it's clear to all concerned that you are on the premises for one reason and for one reason only, you will have closed the door on one more attack on your credibility, integrity, eyesight, competence, etc. When you go to work a game, don't wear any other hat.

Recently, I was asked to draft materials to be included in a "pol-icy pack" for a local basketball officials' association. This posture of "Keeping your objective in mind" was of concern when I wrote:

It is the policy of Board 33 that its members at all times strive for a professional and ethical approach to officiating engagements. Anything less is a disservice to the Board and to fellow members. It is the policy of this Board that its members maintain a posture of total impartiality at all times. To this end, members are requested to review the following policy principles:

- It is the policy of this Board that when you, the member, arrive at a game site to officiate, you are there for one purpose only: to referee a basketball game. You are not there to scout. You are not there to promote any group or special interest. You are not there for any purpose other than that for which you were hired. If the above is clear to everyone, you will have made a good start on the night's assignment.
- It is the policy of Board 33 that members do not accept engagements to officiate when it may *appear* that the relationship of the member to the school involved may affect the member's judgment.
- It is the policy of this Board that the IAABO Manual of Basketball Officiating be closely followed. Specifically, Section 12 (A), regarding statements to media people or others:

  . . . An official should never issue—directly or indirectly—newspaper interviews, statements, at the site where he has or will officiate, nor should he issue statements nor engage in careless discussions regarding coaches, players, fellow officials, students, or institutions. An official is permitted to state the pertinent rule and decision regarding a play in which he was involved.
- It is the policy of this Board that the IAABO Manual of Basketball Officiating, Sections 58-59, be specifically and strictly adhered to by its members:

  After checking the score, officials are required to leave the court together at the end of the game. Officials should neither seek nor avoid coaches, nor permit them to enter their dressing room. They should refrain from any discussion regarding their judgments during the game and should issue no statements to news media, except as to clarification of the rules.
- For the protection of our members it is the policy of Board 33 that flagrant abuses of the rules governing sportsmanship and mistreatment of members be promptly reported, whether such incidents occur during or after the game. Such incidents are to be reported directly to the Board Secretary immediately following the incident. The Board Secretary will present the matter to the Executive Committee. The Executive Committee will then make arrangements for notification of the proper authorities.

Now, you and your partner have dressed, had whatever pre-game conversation you were inspired to, and are about to make your way out to the field or the court. It is at this point, if not before, that you must become aware of the fact that people will be watching you for any signs that you care who wins and who loses the game you are about to officiate.

In basketball, it has been stressed repeatedly, that officials are not to engage in conversation relative to rule interpretations or anything that will or may transpire during the game, unless *both* coaches are present. This is undoubtedly a good practice to follow in other sports as well. A notable exception to this is football. It is common for the football referee and umpire to speak to each head coach separately before the game—logistics dictate this. Also, it is not unusual or improper for a coach to reveal to the officials his "double-triple reverse tackle eligible" play in private before the game for the obvious reason that an unusual play may take some officials by surprise and result in an inadvertent whistle or a flag which must be "eaten." Additionally, such pre-game discussions as often as not occur in the locker room out of public view.

Generally speaking, it is good practice to exchange greetings with the coaches upon entering the field or court. If you have not made the acquaintance of the coach, you will want to know his name and he yours. Other than a very brief exchange of pleasantries, it is not advisable to engage in prolonged conversation with one coach when the other may see and misinterpret your conversation from a distance.

Oftentimes, veteran officials may be well known to both coaches, the players of both teams and both athletic directors. The integrity of these officials and the reputation gained by the manifestation of that integrity over a period of years may be such that both teams and coaches clearly know this official will give them a fair shake and are in a position to respect his decisions. Why then should this official be circumspect about indulging in prolonged banter with either of the coaches? The answer to this is found in the reaction of the spectators. Spectators and strangers to the gym that night may not know the reputation of this official nor are they necessarily going to be aware of the fact that official Jim Dandy has both the undying respect and admiration of the coach of the Mudhens as well as the coach of the Bluebirds. This, then, is what is meant by avoiding even the appearance of partiality. Who ever said officiating was going to be easy?

3

THE LIABILITY TRAP

Officials often ask me: "If thus and such happens during a game I'm refereeing, can I be sued?" The answer to this question is invariably yes.

It has often been said, with much truth, that in America, anyone can sue anyone else for about everything. For example, *The Wall Street Journal* reported that in Indiana a 9-year-old girl filed a lawsuit because there was no toy in her box of Cracker Jacks. Of course, this lawsuit was settled for, as they say, "peanuts," but they don't all end up that way.

In actual practice, litigation is serious and expensive business. I suggest to you that we as officials can no longer afford to hide our collective heads in the sand and think that lawsuits are something that we need not be concerned with. In order to understand what the concept of a lawsuit may mean to any one of us as officials, let's step back a minute and do some spade work.

A physical injury to someone is the most obvious event that we are concerned with as officials in terms of the possibility of a lawsuit arising. In America, the "law" governing liability for bodily injuries is derived largely from the British "common law." The common law consists of cases decided in the courts under a system known as *stare decisis,* or precedent. By comparing the facts of the case to be decided with the facts of earlier cases, a judge forms an opinion as to the appropriate ruling to render. These cases are supposedly decided based on the usage and custom of society. In short, the basic premise is that all persons are held to a certain standard with respect to interactions with others. Stated simply, it is the reasonable expectation of society that on the whole a person pays for his mistakes. Liability to compensate an injured party as a result of one's action or omission, as it were, is determined by standards which have evolved under the law. These standards are known collectively as the "reasonable person" standard.

This standard (in violation) is referred to by the law as negligence. Negligence is actionable under the law in the sense that one who is legally negligent is accountable to another for damages, if the negligence or omission causes an injury. Black's Law Dictionary defines *negligence* as:

> The omission to do something which a reasonable man, guided by those ordinary considerations which ordinarily regulate human affairs, would do, or the doing of something which a reasonable and prudent man would not do. (p. 1184)

Thus, there is a basic question which must be resolved whenever someone is injured: whether the cause of the injury is such that another should be required under the law to compensate the injured party.

Surely, there are many injuries occurring in athletic competition which are largely self-inflicted. Every time someone is injured in an athletic event does not mean someone else is liable for that injury.

As officials, we are responsible for our own negligence. If we fail to meet the standards that the law prescribed and thereby cause another to be injured, we can be held accountable for those injuries.

It can generally be said that there is a basic presumption existing in the law that when an official undertakes to referee or umpire, he in effect is committing himself to accomplishing the task of working the game as would a "reasonably prudent referee." His actions must be reasonable in terms of anticipating negative consequences which would flow from his actions or failure to act in an appropriate situation.

In other words, the long and the short of it is that to minimize your exposure to a costly and expensive lawsuit, you must act as a reasonably prudent official. What is a reasonably prudent official? A reasonably prudent official
- knows the rules that are designed to protect the players,
- knows his or her responsibility in enforcing these rules,
- does not permit anyone to prevent him or her from doing his or her job.

As officials, we are paid for our judgment. We are bound to conduct the game as the rulemakers intended it to be played; fair play in a safe environment for those participating. What this means in practical terms can be seen by reviewing some of the areas where officials have definite responsiblities, spelled out in black and white.

At sea, the captain of the ship is boss. No two ways about it. His word is law, and his first duty is the safety of his passengers. There was a great scene in the movie "Voyage of the Damned " in which the Nazi government attempted to commandeer the ship of the German captain, played by Max Von Sydow, to arrange for the casual disposal of the German Jews on board.

When the diabolical plan was suggested to the captain, he'd have no part of it. His reply was, "they are my passengers." He didn't have to say any more.

As an official, the players are your passengers. The rule book and the approved interpretations give you the authority over the conduct of the game. As is the case with the law of the sea, authority and responsibility go hand in hand. And, although the complete responsibility for the safety of the players cannot, as a practical matter, be relegated to game officials alone, there are many areas where we as officials have a far greater responsibility than any coach, trainer, athletic director, team physician or what have you.

Let's jump back a minute. We have seen that, under some circumstances, action or inaction of the game official under circumstances where he would have been reasonably expected to act or refrain from acting may give rise to that game official's being held legally liable for his actions in a lawsuit. However, the fact that an official may be negligent, and a player is injured during a game, does not mean that this official is legally liable. More is necessary. That is to say, there must be some link between the official's negligence and the injury which occurred. In other words, the injury must have been so related to the action or inaction on the part of the official that it can be said to have been a foreseeable consequence of the action or inaction of the official. The legal concept of a person's actions causing injury to another is referred to as *proximate cause.*

It's not enough that negligence occurs followed by an injury. The injury, in order for one to be held liable, must be a *foreseeable result* of the negligent act or omission. This is proximate cause.

And finally, assuming the presence of negligent conduct, the seriousness of the injury suffered will determine the amount of money awarded. These awards, typically called compensatory damages, are based on both an element of compensation for the injured party to make him whole again for having sustained medical, dental, etc., expenses, and also an amount designated to compensate the victim injured for his "pain and suffering." It is this "pain and suffering" element that often results in jury verdicts and settlements that make newspaper headlines. This is so because juries have a wide latitude in awarding such damages; and how they perceive a particular injured party and the other party in the case, when it comes time to award damages for "pain and suffering," is anybody's guess.

Also, it is a fundamental of the American system of jurisprudence that there may be more than one person or party liable under the law for an injury. Oftentimes one party or entity will be held liable for the negligence of another. This is known as *imputed negligence*. An example of imputed negligence is found in a complex doctrine of the law known as *respondeat superior.*

Based on the theory that an employee represents his employer as his agent, if a court applies *respondeat superior,* the employee's negligence is imputed to the employer. The reasoning behind this is that an employee's actions are actions taken on behalf of his employer. Thus, the employer should be held accountable. As a practical matter, an employee who works for a wage may lack the wherewithall to pay an award of damages to a party who has been severely injured through his negligence. Therefore, by holding his employer liable for damages, two objectives are accomplished. First, the employer is better able to sustain the financial burden of compensating an injured party who was injured through some interaction with the employer's employee. And second, by making the employer liable for the negligence of his employee, it encourages the employer to require his employees to act in a safe and non-negligent manner.

Therefore, as we shall see, the label of a referee or umpire as an employee of a school, league, conference or association could prove to be an extremely significant factor in determining legal liability for an injury to a participant during athletic competition.

In this regard, it's important to note that it is inaccurate to label high school officials, say, automatically as independent contractors rather than employees. In many cases, this distinction is blurred.

Unfortunately, the entire area of the legal status of the official as an independent contractor or employee is fraught with an overriding misconception which is held by many officials and administrators of officiating groups. The misconception takes the form of saying that officials working under any particular system are either independent contractors or employees—for *all* purposes. This is simply not true. To understand why this is not so, we must look at the various situations in which the distinction between an employee and an independent contractor is significant.

Basically, why one would need to know whether anyone is to be classified as an employee or an independent contractor would be to determine the extent of that person's rights or liabilities under the law.

However, a determination that one is an employee for the purpose of taxation, thus requiring his employer to take withholding, social security and the like out of his game fee and submit it to the appropriate governmental authority, is not binding or controlling upon another court or another jurisdiction when the question arises to determine, perhaps, legal liability for negligence.

The point is, an athletic official may be an employee for one legal purpose, and an independent contractor for another legal purpose or situation. And, while a reference to one situation in which the official

An athletic official may be an employee for one legal purpose, and an independent contractor for another legal purpose or situation.

is designated an employee or an independent contractor is or may be of some value in determining the official's status in another context, it is no more than that. Not only do other facts and circumstances affect this determination on a case by case basis, but the purpose of the legal distinction in the particular context will carry much weight in its final determination in a court of law. For, just as we officials on the field or court look to the reason behind the rule as a guide to interpreting a particuar sitation and rendering a decision, the court will often look to the reason and purpose of a rule of law with a view toward giving effect to that purpose by an intelligent, reasonable and fair interpretation of the law.

The distinction between the official as an employee and an independent contractor is necessary to be articulated in several circumstances. In the chapter on officials' associations, we will see how this distinction has been resolved for purposes of taxation of officials. As to liability of officials for injuries, the "employee - independent contractor" distinction is equally as significant.

Why is this so? Damage awards resulting from lawsuits instituted by injured persons are often well beyond the means of all but a very few individuals. If the party whose negligence is the proximate cause of an injury to the claimant is held to be an employee, by the rule of *respondeat superior,* his employer will be liable.

This is not to say that thus the individual official/employee is therefore absolved from a liability when classified as an employee, but as a practical matter, all other things being equal, an injured person may well be able to collect whatever damages he is awarded by way of verdict or settlement, from the employer, which will most often be a school district, league, etc., (or some other institutional employer).

Under another rule of law, many jurisdictions employ the concept of "joint and several liability." This rule specifies that, where more than one party is legally responsible to pay damages, the injured party may recover damages from any one of the responsible persons. There are several different ways for the defendants to apportion their liability, but this does not affect the liability of a school district, for example, to pay the entire amount of the judgment against itself and an official. This practice will vary by jurisdiction and by certain rules governing the liability of various parties.

Certainly, though, it's not hard to see why an institution is better able to sustain a large damage award than an individual with necessarily limited assets.

Additionally, in many jurisdictions, another legal rule comes into play known as "joint contribution among tortfeasors." Under this rule, if an individual official and a school district are alleged liable for an injury, the school district in such a jurisdiction would often file a related lawsuit, called a crossclaim, against the official. In this crossclaim, the school is in effect saying that the official is an independent contractor, responsible to both the injured party and responsible to indemnify, or compensate, the school district if the latter is forced to pay damages as a result of the official's negligence.

Conversely, were the official to be considered an employee, the doctrine of *respondeat superior* would apply, making the school district liable for its employee's negligence.

This situation is analogous to the provisions found in most standard board of education/teacher contracts. School boards typically agree to indemnify their teachers from any lawsuits by paying all legal fees and being responsible for any judgments obtained against their teachers and employees as arising out of their activities in working for the school. Were all officials to receive this protection, they would, of course, be in a much less vulnerable position.

But, for many reasons, it is not realistic to expect that officials will enjoy this protection. In certain situations, they may enjoy this protection, but in others they most assuredly will not.

As to determining the existence of "negligence," a certain amount of confusion exists as to the meanings of the word "legal" in the context of sport and rules of sport. We, as officials, tend to speak of certain actions or tactics or facilities which are either "legal"— meaning they are approved for play and do not conflict with the rules of the sport—or "illegal"—and consequently not permitted under the rules. This is perfectly acceptable terminology. We all use it. But you must guard against assuming that because a particular piece of equipment or a particular tactic is "legal" under the rules, it is "legal" in the sense that use of the tactic or equipment or facilities will automatically immunize you from liability in a lawsuit.

For, as we have seen, whether or not you are liable depends on whether or not you acted as a "reasonable" referee. As a minimum, you must enforce all rules affecting and concerned with players' safety. This means that you must prohibit to the extent possible and penalize when an infraction occurs, any action which is *"illegal"* under the rules which relate to player safety. By this I mean you should look upon what is "illegal" as a minimum standard of care for you to use and not the be all and end all.

For example, the rules of baseball require that a batter wear a helmet. Generally speaking, it is safe to assume that if you permit a player to bat without a helmet and he is struck in the head with a pitched ball, liability could attach to your actions. Strong evidence of your liability could be found in the rule book. Because it is very clear that your contractual duty is, as well as your duty to act as a reasonably prudent umpire, to enforce the rules, and clearly a rule requiring helmets, in light of the way the game is played and the velocity with which pitches are thrown, and the frequency with which batters cannot get out of the way, dictate that strict observance of this rule by umpires is a bare minimum for an umpire to meet the standard of "the reasonably prudent umpire."

If, on the other hand, you are umpiring a baseball game played under professional baseball rules, you may "legally" under those rules permit a batter to wear a cracked helmet. Professional baseball rules, unlike the Federation and NCAA codes, are silent on cracked helmets. However, if the batter gets hit in the head with a fast ball and is injured, you may be liable for permitting him to use unsafe equipment, even though you will have done nothing "illegal" under the rules.

An example of a situation that is "legal" according to the rules, but still could expose you to liability, may be in the area of soccer. For example, the High School Federation version of the rules of soccer provide that casts worn by a player with a broken bone, etc. are permitted if they are covered with soft padding to the satisfaction of the officials. Thus, under these soccer rules, if someone is injured by virtue of a soft part of his body coming into contact with an opponent or a teammate's covered plaster cast, you may not point to the soccer rule book, quote the chapter and verse that says casts are legal if covered with soft padding and be absolved from liability automatically!

LIABILITY INSURANCE

Any discussion of the elements of risk of legal consequences to an individual or institution necessarily has superimposed upon it a discussion of liability insurance. Liability insurance is nothing more than the transferring of the financial risk of a lawsuit or claim to another party. Liability insurance is always controversial when it is first introduced into a new area. For, in some respects, the very same reason why you have it is the same reason why you need it. It will never be resolved to anyone's satisfaction whether liability insurance is in fact a cause or an effect of the rising number of lawsuits filed in all realms of 20th century American endeavor. While it is true that most people today are aware of the fact that insurance companies frequently pay out relatively large sums of money to injured claimants, this does not negate the fact that if you're the one without insurance, a lawsuit could be an extremely costly proposition for you, ranging from a few dollars for legal fees if you are successful in nipping the suit in the bud, to the devastating spector of personal bankruptcy.

The basic problem is a classic case of which came first, the chicken or the egg? If there were only a sporadic lawsuit brought against officials and it was not the norm to expect an injured player or spectator to include the official as a party defendant in a lawsuit, one might hope for the best and carry on the avocation of officiating without any protection in the form of liability insurance. And, in many areas of the country, this is indeed in the picture. In some cases, an official may have a homeowners insurance policy or an umbrella type of coverage which would possibly defend him against a lawsuit arising out of his activities as an official, but, again, this is risky.

On the other hand, since the general expectation today is that people do have insurance, is it not unreasonable to assume that the great rise in the number of lawsuits brought in all areas is predicated in part upon this assumption. If the assumption that you have insurance is not true and you are sued anyway, it may be small comfort to you to think that the injured party didn't know or care that you had no insurance coverage. More importantly, the athlete may be sympathetic to his coach, a buddy and mentor, and for that reason may steadfastly refuse to sue his coach if he is injured in a game. Do you think that the athlete would afford you, the referee or umpire, the same type of sympathetic consideration and decline to sue you? I think not.

Like many other forms of insurance, athletic officials' liability insurance is a better value when you buy it in quantity; as part of a group insurance program. If you have an association, let your insurance broker or agent, in consultation with your attorney, write a policy covering the entire association, or subscribe to one of the national groups that offers a policy which will cover *all* games in whatever sport you're working. Group insurance, by increasing the number of policies sold, decreases the cost and affords you your best value for your insurance dollars spent. There is one large caution, however, when buying liability insurance. Beware of the policy that covers you for liability for only certain types of competition.

For example, some interscholastic athletic associations on a statewide basis have recently been offering policies, or rather, selling policies as part of dues and registration fees to officials which cover the official only in the event that the incident or claim occurs during a high school game. Stay away from this type of insurance, or at least consult with your insurance broker and attorney about purchasing the type of additional coverage that you will need. Your individual member will need to be covered for each and every game they work, whether it is a sandlot baseball game, church league, basketball, Pop Warner football, or the men's touch and beer league on Sunday morning.

Liability insurance is necessary to protect officials working in any type of game on an amateur level. However, it is vital that this type of coverage exist, if at all, for the so-called independent games. For, as we have seen, if a participant or spectator is injured in a high school game or college game and it is alleged that your negligence is such that you should be liable, the injured party always has the school to look to as well as you. In many independent leagues, there is no financially responsible party to sue in the event of a serious injury. You may not have an "employer" as an official with assets (or insurance) sufficient to respond to a judgment of money damages and, the legal duty which you owe to protect the participants may rest upon you alone, depending upon the facts of the particular case. That's why, in independent ball, you need liability insurance more than ever.

The rules for buying liability insurance are basically to treat the purchase as you would any other important purchase; shop around and know what you are buying. Rates are nominal, but for the ten or twenty dollars you spend, know what you're getting in terms of protection. Often, liability policies are marketed in such a way that they are combined with another policy covering medical, dental fee replacement, and other related first party benefits to officials. At this point, it is important to know the difference between liability insurance, which, as we have seen, is designed to protect the policy holder from what insurance people are fond of calling third party claims, and accident or first party insurance. In the language of insurance, you are the first party. The insurance company is the second party. And the person suing you is the third party. Liability insurance covers a claim made by a third party against the insured party. First party coverage such as medical insurance has a different purpose. First party insurance may cover the insured person's medical bills, lost wages, etc. Therefore, when you buy insurance, it's important to know what you are getting for you money.

Also, be aware of two different types of liability policies. Years ago, most liability insurance policies would protect the policy holder against claims arising out of an incident which occurred during the period that the policy was in force. This coverage is known as an occurrence policy. Insurance that covers claims made only during the time the policy is in force is known as claims made policy. Here's why the distinction is important. Let's say that you officiated a basketball tournament game on December 30, 1980. In that game, an incident occurred and a player was injured. Let's also suppose, for purposes of this example, that your officials' liability insurance runs on a calendar year basis, January 1 through December 31.

Now, let's say the injured player decides on November 25, 1981, to make a claim against you alleging that it was your negligence that caused his injury. An "occurrence" policy would cover you on this claim, since the incident in question occurred during the policy period.

Conversely, a claims made type of policy will provide coverage for claims made during the time the policy is in force. Also, this type of policy may provide coverage for certain claims made for a number of months after the policy expires. (This is known as a "tail" in the insurance business.) Generally speaking, the insurance company writing this type of policy could deny you coverage because the claim was not made within the actual policy period. The point is: know what

In independent league ball, you need liability insurance more than ever.

you're buying when signing on with an insurance agent. You can be effectively protected if you are willing to make a few intelligent inquiries. Now, let's explore what happens if you do become involved in a court case.

What does a lawsuit look like?

In most areas, a lawsuit is commenced by the filing of a summons and a complaint. The summons is, of course, the official notice that a party has been sued, and the complaint is the document reciting facts which, if proven in court, the claiming party expects will establish the legal liability of the defending party. The injured party who brings the lawsuit is known as the plaintiff, and the party being sued is known as the defendant.

It should be noted that this proceeding is known as a "civil action," and is a completely separate animal from a criminal action. And, while an act or omission may constitute a crime or misdemeanor under the laws of a given jurisdiction, the same act or omission may also form the basis by which a civil action or lawsuit may be brought. The purpose of a civil action is usually to recover a "judgment" against the defendant, obliging the defendant to pay money to the plaintiff to compensate him for his injuries. The prosecution of a criminal action is brought in the name of the State and usually does not result in the imposition of other than penal sanctions, i.e., fines paid to the State or government and/or jail sentences.

This is an important and fundamental distinction and one which often is lost sight of by officials, as we shall see in the chapter entitled "If You Are Injured." Anyway, there are two things to keep foremost in mind should you be the unhappy and unlucky recipient of a summons and complaint naming you as a defendant. These two things are:

- No one in America today (save, maybe, a resident of the White House), is or has ever had a blanket immunity from being sued. You can be the best official who ever put on a mask or striped shirt, you can act reasonably, prudently and exercise the best judgment and concern, and carry on an entire officiating career without a mistake that would cause you to be legally liable for anyone's injury. This fact will not prevent anyone from suing you. So, accept it if you are served with papers. And,
- Remember that, generally speaking, it is very unwise to offer any remarks to anyone other than your attorney and insurance company, if you have one, regarding the facts which gave rise to the lawsuit.

Once a summons and complaint have been filed, it is necessary that you or your legal representative respond to the allegations contained in the complaint by filing papers of your own with the court. This document is called an Answer. At this point, if you are fortunate enough to have obtained liability insurance coverage, notify your attorney and your insurance carrier. Your insurance carrier will supply an attorney to represent you and be your attorney in defending that lawsuit. The reason why your insurance company supplies the attorney is simple; the insurance company pays his bill and will have to pay any money, up to (and sometimes over) the limits of its policy (with certain exceptions) that is recovered against you; or the insurance company may resolve the claim before or during the trial by settling with the plaintiff for an agreed-upon sum. If the insurance company settles the case before or during the trial, this does not at all mean that it or you are conceding that you are in fact legally liable or that you did anything wrong. It is simply a compromise made by the insurance company to avoid any further expense or legal fees and the risk that what the judge or jury awards the plaintiff may be higher than what the plaintiff is willing to settle for.

Volumes have been written regarding claims and settlements relative to the insurance industry and litigation. For our purposes, you must keep in mind that the insurance company settles or tries cases based on prudent business decisions as to how to best minimize the amount of dollars paid out both in claims and in legal fees. Insurance is a business. There are times when you may not agree with the insurance company's determination. But this again is a business decision, and not an admission of legal liability.

Anyway, once a lawsuit is filed, there are various items which require the attention of the parties during the pendency of the suit; that is, the time after the filing of the suit and before the actual trial of the matter occurs. This period of time may range from several months to several years, depending on the jurisdiction and the number of cases that appear on a court's calendar.

In the meanwhile, modern day court procedures include an activity practiced by attorneys known as pretrial discovery. This discovery period is a time within which attorneys, governed by local rules of court procedures, are permitted to discover facts about the other side's case. This discovery can take the form of *interrogatories*, (written questions concerning the case or the parties which must be answered by the opposing party and sworn to as true to the best of that party's knowledge and belief), depositions upon *oral examination* (oral testimony, under oath, recorded by a stenographic court reporter or recording device, utilizing a question-and-answer format and often held at an attorney's office), physical examinations of injured parties, and examination of documents or other things relating to the case. Attorneys usually use a combination of these devices and, generally, are entitled to "discover" any facts which will help them prepare their case for trial.

While all this is going on, attorneys also use the period between the filing of a lawsuit and the actual call to trial for the filing of *pretrial motions.* Sometimes a party will give testimony in a deposition or by way of answers to interrogatories which will establish and may be deemed an admission of something that the opposing side is trying to prove. When this becomes evident, a party will often make a pretrial motion to remove this aspect of proof from the necessity of being tried. These motions, popularly called summary judgment motions, can result in the resolution of a major aspect of a case such as damages or legal liability or the entire case, without the necessity for a trial at all. A trial of certain issues can be avoided if there is no dispute as to any genuine fact issue in the case and the law is clear. Although this does not happen very frequently in personal injury suits, it is worth remembering.

Having looked at the offensive view of a lawsuit and the basics of establishing a claim from the point of view of the plaintiff, let's take a peek at theories used by defendants to defeat or diminish a plaintiff's claim.

As everyone involved in sports knows, defensive strategy has won many a battle. It's quite the same in the courtroom. Depending, again, on the jurisdiction you are in and the laws of the particular jurisdiction that the court will apply, several defenses may be available to refute a claim of negligence in a personal injury lawsuit. For these purposes, defenses which may be employed in your behalf should you as an official be sued for negligence, can be divided into two broad categories: procedural and substantive. The procedural defenses are technical in nature and relate to the jurisdiction of the court or the place where the trial has been scheduled to be held. We won't waste much time on these here, for the procedural defenses don't really give us an insight into what we need to know as officials. Of the substantive defenses, there are certain prevalent defenses which are utilized in various combinations. These are:

- contributory negligence,
- comparative negligence,
- assumption of the risk,
- statutory immunity, and
- lack of negligence.

The substantive defenses are, of course, complementary to the obvious defense that the injury was not caused by the defendant, but rather by some force over which the defendant had no control. Also, defendants often will claim that any injury to a plaintiff was caused by another party over whom the defendant submitting the defense had no control. There is, naturally, a good deal of overlap in the various defenses. Let's take a look at them, one at a time.

The defense of contributory negligence holds that a plaintiff who contributes to his own injury is barred from recovering damages from a defendant. This aged doctrine has been replaced in, or modified, virtually everywhere in this country, in favor of a more modern theory, known as comparative negligence. Under comparative negligence, it is a defense if the plaintiff was also negligent in his actions. The laws vary from state to state, however. In some states which apply comparative negligence, the monetary award to an injured plaintiff (rather than barring recovery as under contributory negligence), may reduce the amount of recovery to the plaintiff. In some jurisdictions, if a plaintiff's negligence is greater than a defendant's negligence, the plaintiff will recover nothing.

As we have said, the extent to which damages awarded to the plaintiff, if any, will be reduced under comparative negligence, if at all, is a matter of State law. The concept of comparative negligence means that a court or jury will compare the negligence of the plaintiff with negligence of the defendant, and reduce those comparisons to a numerical analysis.

What does this all mean in the event of a lawsuit naming you, the official, as a defendant? Only that comparative negligence is somewhat of a two-edged sword. Although an injured person's own negligence will no longer operate to bar recovery completely, the doctrine of comparative negligence in many jurisdictions will serve to reduce the amount of damages. This is a practical method of spreading responsibility for an injury among the various parties, plaintiff included.

A popular defense in sports injury cases is that of *assumption of the risk*. The theory here is basically that a person who voluntarily participates in an activity knowing that persons sometimes are injured as a result of participating in that activity is barred from recovering damages where injuries are sustained by virtue of such participation. For example, in many team sports, notably football and basketball, it is well known that body contact is an integral part of the game, and when powerful young men are intentionally making contact with each other while moving at a fast clip and performing all the acts indigenous to the game, some injuries are sure to occur.

This defense has been the focal point of most of the outcry against the increase in litigation in the sports area. Athletic administrators, coaches and (most vociferously) manufacturers of athletic equipment such as football helmets, all decry the injured athlete who expects to recover damages since the athlete knew that injuries are "part of the game." What these people often are not aware of is the fact that participants in a sport generally do *not* assume the risk of a coach, referee, or anyone else with whom he comes in contact being negligent, i.e., acting below the standard of care of a reasonable coach, referee, etc., under the circumstances.

All too often, those involved in athletics fail to appreciate the defense of assumption of the risk presupposes that the injured person voluntarily and knowingly entered into the activity. Peer pressure to "make the team" is great for young athletes. Thus, there is always a substantial question in this type of litigation as to how voluntary the participation and how well informed a 12-year old or even a 17-year old athlete is with respect to the risk of participation in interscholastic athletics.

More importantly, comparative negligence statutes have quieted the defense of assumption of the risk in many jurisdictions due to the fact that comparative negligence assesses the injured person's liability as well as that of the defendant's.

The authoritative American Law Institute's Treatise, entitled *Restatement (Second) of Torts,* section 50, b (1965), states:

Taking part in a game manifests a willingness to submit to such bodily contacts or restrictions of liberty as are permitted by its rules or usages. Participating in such a game does not manifest consent to contacts which are prohibited by rules or usages of the game if such rules or usages are designed to protect the participants and not merely to secure the better playing of the game as a test of skill. This is true although the player knows that those with or against whom he is playing are habitual violators of the rules.

Our fourth defense is *statutory immunity.* In many jurisdictions, it is possible to bring a lawsuit for personal injuries against a public entity, such as a municipality which sponsors games through its recreation department, or a school board only under conditions specified by law. At common law, the government could not be sued under the doctrine of sovereign immunity. In recent years, however, this doctrine has been relaxed to the extent that most states have passed legislation permitting lawsuits against an entity or division of a government under circumstances where the legislature decides that injuires are serious enough to make it desirable as a matter of public policy for the State to share in the cost, if the public entity is in fact liable under the principles of the law of negligence.

However, the immunity that school boards and municipalities may enjoy may in some cases depend on whether the activity in which the injury occurs is considered proprietary, in the case of an activity that is income producing as opposed to purely governmental activities. These regulations are complex and of course vary widely from state to state. Enough to say that under certain circumstances you, as an official, may be affected should the school or league whose games you officiate prevail in a claim of immunity from suit. Though the school may be immune from suit, you, the official, generally will not be!

Two lawsuits which were brought by injured high school wrestlers about 10 years and 5,000 miles apart illustrate well the difference between this type of litigation then and now. In the earlier case,[1] the plaintiff's opponent was attempting to pin plaintiff by employing alternating "half-nelsons" in an effort to roll plaintiff into a pin position. As a result of this action, the wrestlers ended up in a corner of the main mat near the mats intersecting with some smaller side mats. The referee noticed that one of the side mats had become separated from the main mat, exposing the hardwood floor. While the referee attempted to correct this situation by replacing the side mat, plaintiff's opponent allegedly placed a "full-nelson" hold upon the plaintiff. This hold was held upon the plaintiff for a period of, depending upon which witness is believed, 1 to 10 seconds. Thereafter, there was an almost simultaneous end-of-period signal, the referee's whistle, and a final lunge by the plaintiff's opponent after which he broke the hold. Plaintiff was rendered quadraplegic due to a severance of a major portion of his spinal cord.

Suit was brought against the two competing school districts, but, not the referee. Instead, the plaintiff was content to let his fortunes in the lawsuit rest upon the success of his claim against the school district who hired the referee; the reason being, apparently, to sue the party with the "deep pocket," as opposed to the "little guy," the referee hired to work the match. As it turned out, the referee had no insurance coverage of his own.

Nonetheless, the referee, although he was not sued, was the "star" of the show in the lawsuit to recover $500,000 against the two competing school districts. This is so because the complaint stated that the school districts were negligent because the referee was negligent and the referee was their agent. The plaintiff in this case cited the legal principle that the school district owed a duty to protect students participating in interscholastic wrestling, and that this duty consisted of anticipating reasonably foreseeable dangers and guarding against these dangers by providing for supervision, in the form of referees, that was non-negligent.

The *Restatement (Second) of Agency,* Section 214 (1957), states that:

A master or other principal who is under a duty to provide protection for or to have care used to protect others or their property and who confides the performance of such duty to a servant or other person is subject to liability to such others for harm caused to them by the failure of such agent to perform the duty.

There are three forms of the duty of protection. First, a person may have a duty to protect another which can be performed either by exercising care personally in protecting the other or by exercising care in the employment of an independent contractor to protect the other. Secondly, there may be a duty to protect another at all hazards, a duty which is not fulfilled unless the other is protected and which is not satisfied by the use of care. This duty normally exists only when undertaken by contract. Thirdly, one may have a duty to see that due care is used in the protection of another, a duty which is not satisfied by using care to delegate its performance to another but is satisfied if, and only if, the person to whom the work of protection is delegated is careful in giving the protection. In this third class, the duty of care is non-delegable.

In this case, the complaint stated that the school districts, acting through their agent, the referee, were negligent in:

- Failing to adequately supervise the contestants;
- Allowing his attention to be diverted from the actions of the contestants;
- Allowing an illegal and dangerous hold to be applied;
- Failing to immediately cause the illegal and dangerous hold to be broken;
- Allowing the illegal and dangerous hold to be prolonged for a substantial period of time;
- Violating the provisions of the applicable wrestling rule book.

At the close of the presentation of evidence by each side in a lawsuit, the judge will give the jury, if there is one, his "charge." This is a statement of what the law is to the jury so they may decide what the facts are and apply those facts to the law. This was a portion of the judge's charge relating to the referee:

The defendant school districts owed a duty to the student participants in the wrestling match to exercise reasonable and ordinary care to protect them from injury during the wrestling match. Under the evidence in this case, the only person who was carrying out this duty of the defendants was the referee, John Smith. (sic) Accordingly, the question of whether or not the defendant's school districts were negligent is narrowed down as to whether or not the referee . . . was negligent during the course of the wrestling match. If you find that the referee was not negligent, then the school district defendants were not negligent.

In the end, the jury found for the defendant, concluding in effect that the referee's negligence, if any, was not the proximate cause of plaintiff's injury.

Just to give you an idea of energy expended on these sorts of suits, consider a few of the salient details.

- The trial took 20 days.
- 38 witnesses testified.
- The statement of facts alone in the case consisted of over 2,300 pages.

Naturally, the plaintiff appealed from the verdict. The State's Supreme Court upheld the appeal and ordered a new trial. Interestingly, one of the reasons why the plaintiff brought this appeal was that he contended that one of the defense attorneys improperly remarked to the jury that the plaintiff was being aided financially through insurance and that a verdict for the plaintiff would be so burdensome to the schools that it would cause the discontinuance of many school athletic programs. At any rate, the case was settled before the new trial was to occur. The case is now over, but the lesson lives on.

Ten years later, across the country, another wrestling referee was not so fortunate as to avoid being named a defendant as a result of his actions during a wrestling match he was working.[2]

In 1975, a high school wrestling official was once again involved, this time as a defendant, in major litigation as a result of a wrestler becoming paralyzed after competing in a wrestling match. The allegation was that an illegal "stack" hold was employed, exerting vertical pressure on the plaintiff's neck, causing the crippling injury.

Who was legally culpable for this injury? The injured wrestler claimed that the referee was guilty of negligence such as was sufficient to proximately cause the injury in that he did not discharge his duties as referee properly. How a plaintiff goes about proving these allegations will necessarily focus on two fact areas. First, it is necessary to establish, often by testimony of eye witnesses, the actual facts surrounding the incident — what did happen in this particular case? Secondly, it is of course necessary in most cases for an injured plaintiff to elicit testimony and other evidence indicating that the defendant, whether it be a referee, a coach or anyone else, failed to discharge the legal duty that he owed to the plaintiff, thereby causing his injury. Thus, once the facts of the referee's actions are proven, it is necessary to prove to the court that those actions or inactions were something less than would have been done by a reasonably prudent referee, and that this in fact caused the injury complained of.

Invariably, an injured person will retain one or more expert witnesses who have the knowledge and background to give testimony as to what a reasonably prudent referee would have done given the circumstances of the case. Naturally, if you are involved as a referee-defendant, your attorney will similarly retain expert witnesses who, hopefully, will be prepared to testify that you did in fact act as a reasonably prudent referee and/or your actions or inactions were not the proximate cause of the injury. How would an expert witness employed by an injured athlete go about convincing a jury that you, the referee, were negligent in your duties? Let's take a look at a written report from one such expert, paraphrased from the 1975 case in which a high school wrestler was seriously injured, allegedly as a result of an illegal "stack" hold.

In the second period the "referee's" position was assumed where both wrestlers were on all fours, side by side, with plaintiff's right arm over his opponent's back and extending under his stomach. The left hand grasped the opponent's left elbow. When ready, the referee blew his whistle to begin. During this second period each wrestler scored various points. However, during the point scoring, the opponent got the plaintiff into a "stacked" position. That is, the plaintiff was on all fours. The opponent grabbed the plaintiff's left arm and pulled it under the plaintiff's crotch and at the same time applied terrible vertical pressure with his forearm on the back of the plaintiff's neck. The opponent's purpose was to yank and push at the same time to cause the plaintiff's head to be forced into the mat, the legs going over in a somersault attitude with such momentum and force that the plaintiff would have ended up on his back with the opponent on top of him in hopes of a pin. Before the opponent could accomplish the throw, the plaintiff was able to drag himself to the edge of the mat and time was called. Both boys went to the center of the mat and assumed the "referee's" position. This ended the second period. Mr. Referee did not say anything to the opponent in spite of his potentially dangerous hold.

After a few seconds, the third period started and now the opponent was on top. Both boys went for hand control, body control, etc., until the opponent maneuvered the plaintiff into a "stacked" position. The referee did not warn the opponent of this illegal hold. The two boys went through the motions for control until the opponent, who for the second time during this third period had the plaintiff in a stacked position, only this time the opponent had such a firm grip on the plaintiff's wrist and such verticle (sic) pressure on his neck, like in a vise, that the pain to the neck was so excruciating, the plaintiff could only grit his teeth, let out groans of pain and *try to signal Mr. Referee with his eyes*, (emphasis supplied) but was ignored and got no whistle response from the referee to stop the match thereby subjecting the plaintiff to an unreasonable risk of harm.

Before the plaintiff could get out of this hold he was flipped over with such force that he ended up on his back and was pinned. Mr. Referee signaled the pin. The opponent got up and went back to the center of the mat and waited for the plaintiff to get up, come to the center of the mat, as is the custom, and shake the winner's hand. But when Mr. Referee signaled to Gene to get up he saw he could not move. When the referee went over to Gene to see what was wrong, Gene was in such pain and shock that in a whisper he told the referee he couldn't move. The referee called Mr. Coach over and within a short time the First Aid Squad, who were on duty for the matches in anticipation of injuries that this body-contact sport could/did cause, came over and applied a splint type stretcher under Gene. He was then placed on a rolling stretcher, put into an ambulance and taken to the Dover General Hospital in Dover, N.J.

On Saturday, December 17, 1975, in the Main Town Regional High School, plaintiff wrestled against opponent from Redmont High School. During the second and third periods, the opponent got the plaintiff into an illegal hold by putting vertical pressure on the plaintiff's neck instead of lateral pressure, thereby causing a serious injury. Mat judges were not used to aid and/or assist the referee in the wrestling tournament on December 27, 1975.

Mrs. Amy Jones, wife of Richard Jones, takes her son Gene to State College in New Jersey four days out of every week and remains waiting for him to pursue his education from 9 A.M. to 12 noon.

Gene is now a quadraplegic as a result of unreasonable care by the people in charge.

DISCUSSION, EVALUATION, ANALYSIS AND OPINION

We have here a sports program with play and protective equipment available for and exposed to the use of high school students with various people in charge to conduct this competitive program. In the field of teaching sports' activities and conducting tournaments relative to these sports, planning, safety control and foreseeability must be considered where there is a possibility of injury to any contestant.

It is the responsibility of all people involved, including all coaches who attended this tournament, who arranged dangerous body contact sports to see to it that the students are properly prepared, qualified and supervised to participate in these sports in accordance with the rules and regulations relating to such games and contests. Where there is a deviation of the accepted standards/rules and regulations pertaining to any competitive sport, a danger and a hazard to the participants is created. The behavioral patterns of young people in high school sports, goaded on to win by their schools and coaches, are so unpredictable that the people in charge should always provide full safety measures regarding qualified personnel, constant safety instruction, safe equipment, injury awareness, foreseeability and, above all, for the coaches and schools not to push their charges beyond the limitations of their ability. And for their team members to be considerate of their opponent.

During the course of his wrestling training he was taught the "stack" position. As a matter of fact, Gene was in a cradle hold when he experienced terrible pain in the neck and shoulders as a result of this type of action and the referee took no steps to stop it during the meet just the week before.

The "stack" position is very much like the double arm bar (p.44, 1974-1975, National Federation of Wrestling rule book), only worse. Not only does the man on top (other man on all fours) have his arm on top of the back of the other man's neck, but also has a grip on his wrist which is attached to the arm coming under the crotch. Vertical pressure is then exerted on the man's neck, the under-the-crotch arm is yanked at the same time, causing the person (on all fours) to whip through the air in a somersault attitude where the neck can be forced to a point where it just won't give any more, and break. Such a situation existed when Gene Jones was injured.

In the National Federation Wrestling rule book, 1974-1975, Page 10, Article 11, it states:

"The user of a potentially dangerous or illegal hold shall be cautioned by the referee, in order to prevent possible injury. The referee shall stop such holds if possible before they reach the dangerous state. If the hold were illegal, the offender must be penalized."

The "stack" is potentially dangerous because of the possibility of injury. It must be broken immediately! Yet on December 27, 1975, Gene Jones was forced into this hold three times. The first time he managed to crawl to the edge of the mat. The second time he managed to crawl to the edge of the mat. On neither of these occasions was opponent warned or prevented from executing this dangerous hold. Now he could go "gung-ho" to win his match. He threw all cautions to the wind, and in spite of the fact that the plaintiff gave out cries of distress, he ignored them and with only his thought of winning (not sportsmanship) pinned plaintiff to the mat after performing an illegal hold.

However, when the opponent applied such excruciating pain to the plaintiff's neck when he had him in a "stack" position, exacerbation took over and all he could do was let out cries of pain, exhibit a pained expression on his face and try to signal with his eyes to the referee that he was in trouble.

It is my opinion, that this being the case, Mr. Referee should have foreseen the potential danger of this hold, and as the rule book states, "it must be broken immediately."

All the people responsible for conducting this wrestling tournament, including all participating coaches, were negligent because mat judges were not provided on December 27, 1975. One of the main purposes of two (2) mat judges is designed to minimize human error. Human error by the referee and/or human error by anyone of the wrestlers. Mat judges may enter the wrestling area to stop a potentially dangerous situation.

These mat judges could have seen/observed the distress of Gene Jones was in and stopped the match immediately. Perhaps they might not have, but the laws of probability were not even given a chance, thereby causing a serious injury to Gene Jones. And, if a mat judge did call "time," the "stack" hold would have been broken immediately, the judges and referee would have met at the edge of the mat and discussed the point of disagreement.

Again, Gene Jones would have had a "breather," his coach would have noticed him again rubbing his neck and taken steps to look as to his discomfort.

When a body part is forced beyond the limit of normal range of movement, the wrestler applying this hold shall be cautioned against forcing it into an illegal position. Contestants, coaches and referees should know the danger of these holds and foresee/anticipate the dangers of injury from these holds. By deviating from this responsibility, all the people involved/responsible for conducting this tournament were in violation of the rules and regulations as set forth by the National Federation of State High School Associations and the State Interscholastic Athletic Association.

The truth of the matter is that you can take every precaution recommended in this book and then some, in addition to acting as reasonable as reasonable can be in terms of fulfilling your duties as a referee or umpire, and still, you could be sued!

Prior to the match, the referee, in addition to the respective participating coaches, had a duty to warn against the use of harzardous excessive and/or illegal holds. This was not done. Rules and regulations might properly be included under safety devices for there is an obligation to establish rules for safety purposes as well as to carry out the rules so established.

Think these same accusations couldn't be made against you in a court of law? Guess again. The truth of the matter is that you can take every precaution recommended in this book and then some, in addition to acting as reasonable as reasonable can be in terms of fulfilling your duties as a referee or umpire, and still, you could be sued! But do yourself a favor: take every precaution to protect yourself anyway. Narrow the odds in your favor. **Read on.**

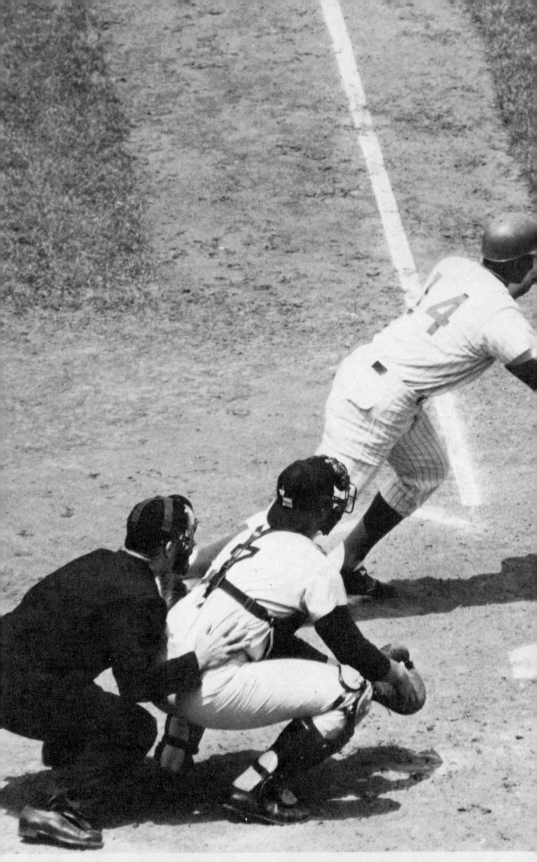

4

CHECK-UP FOR BASEBALL AND SOFTBALL UMPIRES

First of all, as the old umpire once said, "Don't park in the space that says 'Reserved for Umpires.'" Those who ignored this adage in the past were often greeted with sand in the crankcase, sugar in the gas tank or slashed tires at game's end. But seriously, folks, amateur baseball being what it is, in most areas you will find yourselves dressing out of the trunk of the car. Although a surprising number of our umpires may disagree, it's always a smart idea to park your car as close as possible to that of your partner's. Not only does it give you an opportunity to have your pre-game discussions together, but facilitates entering and leaving the field together. For reasons we'll get into, these minutia of procedure are a must. When I'm working baseball, if my partner parks a distance from me, I get in the car and go to him, if it is at all physically possible.

Somehow or other, in baseball and softball more than in any other sports, umpires have a habit of dressing and strolling onto the field, on the way chatting with anyone who's around, including the coaches, and casually waiting for the partner to appear. This does little to give the impression that the umpires are a team. However, many excellent umpires continue this practice.

Speaking of the habits of umpires, another of my favorites is the situation in which you are assigned by position to work a baseball game and your position is the bases. Game time is, say, 2:00 o'clock, and you're there in the 1:30 area. You proceed to get dressed for the bases. Time passes and it's 1:35. It's 1:40. It's 1:50. It's 1:53. All of a sudden you ask yourself: I wonder if I'm working a one-man game today?

So, dedicated as you are, you strip down to the bare essentials and begin to dress up again; this time to work the plate. You wiggled into your chest protector, anchored your cup and shin guards, bent over to remove your spikes (at your age you didn't think you could bend down that far from a standing position!), and now you're just tying the last of the shoelaces on your plate shoes, when in walks your partner one minute before game time. In the meanwhile, the coaches are jumping up and down looking at their watches and wondering why the umpires are late.

At this point, either one of two things happens: your partner says "Oh, I see you've got it, stay the way you are." Or, he says "I think I was assigned to the plate for this game. I'll be with you in a minute." In the interim, you begin your Gypsy Rose Lee act once again, divesting yourself of the 50 pounds of equipment, and your partner, who may use a balloon and always walks around with shin guards on, is ready to go. Then, to add insult to injury, he trots out on the field and joins the coaches. Now, the three of them, the two coaches and your partner, are looking at their watches waiting for you because you were late. Nice, huh?

Don't let it happen! If you think you're going to make yourself look good at your partner's expense, you're in the wrong business. Now, if it's 5 minutes before game time and your partner hasn't yet arrived, you had better walk out onto the field and explain to the coaches that there may be some delay, that you're waiting for so-and-so.

Assuming, however, that everything goes according to schedule, you and your partner arrive with ample time to dress, it is imperative that you enter the field together in a businesslike manner and present yourselves as a team. If you don't think this has an effect on the players, coaches and spectators, you haven't been around very long. Ten minutes or so before game time is not a time for swapping "war stories" with coaches or trying to make sure that everyone has a list of your open dates (since you're booking them so fast you wouldn't want to leave anyone out). It's a time for you to begin doing your job!

The basic procedure, assuming infield practice has been completed (which it never has; the only time they finish infield practice by game time is when you and your partner are late), is as follows: you will, in most cases, want to proceed directly to home plate for the traditional pregame meeting with the captains and/or coaches to exchange line-up cards and go over ground rules and/or special rules for the day's game. If the coaches appear and it's an independent type of game, write down the names of the coaches or managers as they introduce themselves. Do this in their presence. Make sure they get your name and don't assume that everyone knows Bill Macho, the great umpire. As in any sport you're working, an affable but reserved approach works best. Although personalities and relationships differ, most coaches and captains will at least start off with a modicum of respect for an umpire who comports himself in such a fashion as to show respect, and to have a sincere interest in contributing to a good game. Of course, if there are special rules, curfews, or other items which differ from whatever rule book you're playing that day, now is the time that these should be spread around. It certainly isn't cricket, in neither baseball nor softball, to change the rules in the middle of the game, as they say. Make it clear to both teams what set of rules you understand that they're playing. Among professional rules (we oldtimers used to call that "straight baseball"), NCAA, National Federation, Pony League, Babe Ruth League, Little League and other variations in baseball alone, you had better be straight on whose book you're going by, even if you've never seen the book before.

No matter what special rules you're playing, remember that it would not be wise for you to permit the waiver of any rule where a safety factor is involved. For example, don't accept a manager telling you "We have a league rule where batters don't have to wear helmets." If one of the players turns up with a very bad case of fractured skull, the "league rule" won't help you one bit.

At the pre-game conference of captains and/or coaches and umpires, note well any complaints that are made to you regarding the condition of the field and hazards such as broken glass, holes large enough to accommodate a human foot, and protruding sprinkler valves or drainage pipes. Also, take note of automobiles or abandoned football blocking instruction equipment which may be languishing in the outfield or in live ball territory down the foul lines. Since the vast majority of our fields on the sub-high school level and a substantial number of our high school and even college fields are unfenced, you will want to provide for removal of any of these obstacles that have the potential for causing a player to be injured. Additionally, for those items which cannot be moved, you will want to make sure that a suitable ground rule is made known to both coaches *before* the first pitch.

At this point, softball umpires want to make sure that the bats to be used by the teams are not dented and that they comply with the requirements regarding handles and safety grips. Also, the base umpire will want to check out the borings for the bases, especially in the case of the flat bags which are used and sometimes tethered to a rod inserted into the ground. Make sure the rod does not protrude, so a danger to players is prevented. Softball catchers under ASA rules are required to wear chest protectors. Do not, of course, permit a catcher to disregard this requirement. Also, a competent softball umpire will not permit the wearing of jewelry by any player as this is prohibited under the ASA code.

If there is an exposed sprinkler pipe, get someone to cover it up; if there is an automobile, get someone to move it. Although it may be bothersome and you may encourage some griping and unpleasantness before the game, remember this, if someone is injured, you as the umpire may very well be asked to pay.

A frequent and aggravating problem in baseball, due to the open air arrangement of most fields, is the encroachment of spectators into live ball areas. This is something that always has been and always will be a source of difficulty. You must emphasize to coaches (and athletic directors, if available), that it is incumbent upon them to make arrangements to supervise the spectators in such a way that they will not be standing or seated or walking bicycles in an area where the baseball, if it goes there, is still in play. If you don't, once again an injured party may well try to send the bill to you in the form of a lawsuit.

This will, despite your vigilance before the game, often require vigilance during the game, as spectators tend to inch their way again onto the field. Be wary of infants, children with bicycles, and the retiree who pushes a beach chair out of his van and proceeds to get close to the action 5 feet from the left field foul line. All of these people represent trouble for you with a capital "T."

As to equipment, the guiding principle is "a place for everything and everything in its place." Let's take a look at specifics regarding equipment.

HELMETS

With baseballs sailing over home plate at speeds upwards of 90 miles per hour, the batter's helmet is a truly important piece of equipment. Sometimes, when you get an argument from a player who wants to wear a cracked helmet or one without required earflaps, it may cause you wonder which is harder, the helmet or the player's head. I venture to say that for the ability to withstand the impact of a baseball sailing at high speed, the helmet will in almost all cases win out. For this reason, you , the umpire, had better be sure that participants in baseball or softball wear helmets with all the necessary features and at all times when required by rules to do so.

As to baseball, High School Federation and NCAA College rules governing the wearing of protective head gear are virtually identical.The colleges require double earflap helmets to be worn by all batters and runners, with the special proviso written into the rules that "helmets that are badly cracked, split or broken shall not be worn." By way of penalty, college rules provide that a batter or runner shall be declared out if not wearing the proper helmet.

High School Federation rules also specify that the catcher, in addition to the batter and all runners, wears a head protector. Ear-flaps are required for batters' and runners' helmets and the high school code goes on to say that "the head protector shall be a type which has safety features equal to or greater than those provided by the full plastic cap with padding on the inside." Also, in high school baseball, a batter or runner will be declared out for deliberately removing his head protector during playing action.

In both sets of codes, the requirement that all helmets be NOC-SAE approved will be in full effect beginning with the 1985 season. Although these rules are clear cut and have been in now long enough in their present forms so there is little excuse for teams not having the proper helmets, do not accept any excuses whatever in games where either High School Federation or NCAA College rules apply. If a team does not have enough helmets or proper helmets, they will borrow those from the other team. If this alternative is not available because the other team refuses to loan them, do not play the game. DO NOT PLAY THE GAME! In this unusual situation you must take charge to protect yourself.

Professional baseball rules, understandably, provide a "grandfather" clause, because these rules are intended for use by professional leagues. For amateur leagues using professional rules, the only requirement would seem to be found in Rule 1.16(a): "All players shall use some type of protective helmet while at bat."

The High School Federation requires that the baseball catcher wear a cup, a chest protector, and shin guards. Make sure all of these things are in place. Of course, the cup you'll have to ask about. In any event, it's a good idea to confirm the catcher's equipment with the catcher himself in the presence of your partner.

Softball umpires should be aware that rules specifically prohibit any ". . . item judged dangerous by the umpire." Casts, exposed jewelry, i.e., watches, bracelets, neckwear and large or loop-type earrings may never be worn.

Even a relatively insignificant item that at first blush you wouldn't think would constitute a safety hazard, may be the topic of a lawsuit. For example, most codes of rules state that the pitcher shall not wear any white undershirt. This is so the ball will not be effectively hidden from the batter or camouflaged by the appearance of a white undershirt which mirrors the color of the ball upon delivery. If you ignore the rule and a batter gets hit, even with a change-up, he may use your failure to enforce the rule as a weapon against you!

Of all the major rules codes, the professional baseball rule book gives the strongest and best provision to define the umpire's duty before the game. Rule 3.01(a) states:

Before the game begins the umpire shall . . . require strict observance of all rules governing implements of play and equipment of players.

WEATHER AND FIELD CONDITIONS

They say everybody talks about the weather, but nobody does anything about it. As an umpire, you may have to! Baseball and softball, more than any other sports, seem to be beset with difficult problems brought about by weather. Baseball and softball umpires are often faced with two big question marks concerning the onset of either inclement weather or darkness during the game. These question marks are, simply stated, "When and if."

The point in time at which you, the umpire, are in control of the game is important and this is one of those times when you had better know which set of rules you are playing under. In baseball there is a time before the game when the decision of whether or not to play because of inclement weather is the responsibility of the home team. There does come a time, though, as we shall presently see, when this responsibility shifts to the plate umpire.

In professional baseball rules, Rule 4.01 states the following:

Unless the home club shall have given previous notice that the game has been postponed or will be delayed in starting, the umpire, or umpires, shall enter the playing field five minutes before the hour set for the game to begin and proceed directly to home base where they shall be met by the managers of the opposing teams. In sequence:
- First, the home manager shall give his batting order to the umpire-in-chief, in duplicate.
- Next, the visiting manager shall give his batting order to the umpire-in-chief, in duplicate.
- The umpire-in-chief shall make certain that the original copies of the respective batting orders are identical, and then tender a copy of each batting order to the opposing manager. The copy retained by the umpire shall be the official batting order. The tender of the batting order by the umpire shall establish the batting orders. Thereafter, no substitutions shall be made by either manager, except as provided in these rules.
- As soon as the home team's batting order is handed to the umpire-in-chief, the umpires are in charge of the playing field and from that moment they shall have sole authority to determine when a game shall be called, suspended or resumed on account of weather or the condition of the playing field.

The National Federation High School baseball rules aren't quite as specific as the professional version.
Rule 4, Section 1, Article 2, states that:

The home coach shall decide whether the grounds and other conditions are suitable for starting the game. NOTE: After the game starts, the umpires are sole judges as to whether conditions are fit for play, . . .

NCAA College Rules cover the situation this way:

Rule 4:
Pregame procedures
Fitness of field

Section 2.a.
The coach or director of athletics (or his representative) of the host institution shall decide as to whether a game shall not be started because of unsatisfactory conditions of weather or playing field, except for the second game of a double header.

b. Should bad weather or unfit conditions prevail during a game, the umpire-in-chief shall be the sole judge as to the suspension, resumption or termination of play.

Section 4.
Ten minutes before the scheduled starting time, the umpire-in-chief shall conduct the pregame meeting with the representatives of the opposing teams, at which time the home team and visiting team shall deliver their respective batting orders in duplicate to the umpire-in-chief. After determining that the copies of each batting order are identical, the umpire shall retain a copy of each and submit the duplicate to the opposing team's representative. The umpire is now officially in charge of the game.

In softball, Rule 5, Sec. 2, clearly states:

The Fitness Of The Ground For A Game Shall Be Decided Solely By The Plate Umpire.

This provision would seem to indicate that it is the plate umpire and not the home team who decides whether a game will be started at all if weather interferes. While it is true that the playability of the field may always be an issue to be decided by the plate umpire in baseball, a decision to start the game still, as we shall see, rests with the home club, and that decision having been made, the umpire then would direct the home club to render the field playable. If this cannot or is not done, the game may then be called.

These details may seem unimportant at first blush. But, remember this, if someone is injured due to field or weather conditions, the code of rules under which you are umpiring may be an important factor in a court's determination of your liability for those injuries. In other words, a reasonably prudent umpire discharges his responsibilities under the rules. Therefore, he must know and intelligently apply the rules of the particular game he is working. If the rules place a responsibility on him, he must not abdicate that responsibility by deferring to a coach, athletic director or whomever. Do not neglect this aspect of your game.

Sounds easy, doesn't it? The two big question marks referred to earlier, "when?" and "if?" mean, in simple terms, that it is you the umpire (and I mean both umpires, consulting with each other), who must take responsibility for deciding if the weather, either due to rain or darkness, poses a danger to the participants. Or, if the condition of the field poses a danger to the participants, either have the field made playable, or do not play. In short, act as a reasonable umpire!

You should understand, however, that you had better err in this department on the side of suspending play if there is any question in your mind. This is so because, as we have stressed throughout this book, what in your judgment is reasonable may not be the same reasonable the jury comes up with. Therefore, you want to be conservative and avoid unnecessary chances — if your objective is to protect yourself.

Don't be a "good Joe." Trying to get in just one more inning may help get you into a lawsuit.

It wouldn't be right to leave the topic of inclement weather without discussing the one weather situation that constitutes an exception to this reasoning process you as an umpire would have to go through in the event of a weather problem. This is lightning. If you are playing an outdoor game, and you see lightning anywhere, suspend play immediately. If you are the plate umpire, suspend play immediately and don't take any nonsense from anyone. Retreat without delay to your car or room. If you are the base umpire, don't let another pitch go in or another play be made. Call time immediately. Race to home plate and inform your partner. Don't take any chance whatever with lightning!

It, of course, will often be necessary to determine whether or not there is sufficient maintenance and grounds keeping personnel and supplies to render the field playable after it had become unplayable. In most situations, even on a scholastic and collegiate level, it is likely that there may not be facilities and manpower for purposes of restoring a field to a playable condition immediately after a rain delay. In this case, you have no choice. But remember this, if you do have the wherewithall to prepare the field, you must undertake to inspect and examine the field to make sure that whatever the home team or game management has done, it has had the effect of making the field in fact safe and playable. Don't take their word for it. Inspect, make corrections by directing the personnel to add more sand here or close the gap there, but have them do whatever is necessary. In the alternative, call the game. If you permit the game to resume *assuming* that the ground crew or custodians have thrown some sand around and the field looks fine, your assumption may not be correct, you could be just as legally liable as if you failed to stop the game when you should have, in the event that a player is seriously injured.

No matter what special rules you're playing, remember that it would not be wise for you to permit the waiver of any rule where a safety factor is involved.

OTHER SAFETY FACTORS

In the unlikely event that a player is rendered unconscious during a game played under National Federation Baseball Rules, high school umpires know that the player may not return to playing action *that same day*, without the written authorization of a physician. Who is given responsibility to enforce this provision? The umpires, of course.

However rare this occurrence might be, it would be even more rare to find a situation where a high school baseball player was knocked out during a game *and* a physician happened to be in attendance. Moreover, it is highly unlikely that any physician would give his approval to a player who suffered the effect of concussion to resume competition on the basis of a cursory examination at the field.

In fact, it is the opinion of some medical authorities that any loss of consciousness suffered by a player indicates a need for observation, preferably in a hospital, for at least 24 hours.[1]

Therefore, it is not unreasonable to take the position that an unconscious baseball player may not return to play the game, or during the second game if it is a doubleheader. If you, as an umpire, permit him to again participate, you are risking being held liable if his condition should deteriorate.

GAME CONTROL

As to discipline, sometimes it's easy to determine when you must eject a player or coach, and sometimes it's not. It's doubly hard for us working baseball or softball because there's no such thing as a 15-yard penalty; nor can you march to the free throw line to shoot technical fouls. All you can do is grin and bear it, or lower the boom and launch the offender off the field or from the bench.

Additionally, many of the players and coaches operating in the scholastic amateur baseball leagues and in the collegiate ranks have become so accustomed to the major league type of theatrical argument appearing nightly on the television screen that they take such behavior as appropriate models to use on the sandlot, the high school field and the college diamond.

Therefore, baseball presents problems in this respect that the other sports do not. Obviously, you must not permit anyone to charge you like a raging bull only to be stopped by your midriff. It stands to reason that such behavior resulting in bumping, being physical, is an aggressive act which violates your person and riles the crowd, must be dealt with appropiately and immediately.

Similarly, you can't afford to keep around any coaches or players who feel that the only way to impress upon the spectators the stupidity of your calls is to toss objects such as bats, shin guards, or towels onto the field of play.

Finally, don't permit anyone to refer to your parentage or sexual proclivities in other than accurate terms within earshot of others. This should be self-evident. You must distinguish between a player expressing his opinion to you that you have just made a !#! call and a player expressing his opinion to you that you are in fact a !#!. In the latter case, you must eject the player immediately.

It's unfortunate that, in baseball more than any other interscholastic sport, we are often operating in both varsity and underclass ball with a situation wherein there is only one coach, i.e., faculty member, or who is physically with the team at a given field site. This is so because many schools carry only one coach per squad and play varsity and JV ball at the same time, with the JV team going to a different field at the home team site for the purpose of playing both games simultaneously. In New Jersey, the State Interscholastic Athletic Association has promulgated a directive to its officials in all sports to the following effect: If it is necessary to eject a coach in a game when there is no other coach or faculty member present to supervise the players, the coach may not be dismissed from the field and/or bench as may be provided by the rules of the particular sport, but rather must be directed to take a seat in the stands or bleachers in order that he may supervise his team.

This, of course, is a particularly harsh doctrine in terms of its implication for the game officials. What they are saying is, if the coach is unable to control himself to the extent that you have to eject him, you still must keep him around so he is in a position to be able to supervise. Yet, the very purpose of ejecting a coach is to bar further contact with the team. Thus, at least in one state, if you have the unfortunate occurrence of ejecting a coach and there is no substitute member of the faculty to take up the cudgel, you are in the unfortunate position of having to assume responsibility for diminishing a significant element of supervision over the players.

By contrast, in at least one neighboring state, the state interpreter for officials has ruled that in a circumstance such as the one outlined, if there were no adult coach or faculty member to supervise the team, the officials were directed to forfeit the game in the event of the ejection of the only remaining coach or faculty member.

In fairness, the New Jersey State Interscholarstic Athletic Association did provide that a coach, once ejected under circumstances where he is required to remain in the spectator area to exercise supervision over his team, should he again commence to make a pest of himself to the point where he persists in unsportsmanlike behavior, the officials are then authorized to declare a forfeit.

5

CHECK-UP FOR BASKETBALL OFFICIALS

A cynic once suggested that the basketball referees' rating form should have two check-off boxes:

☐ Took the game away from the players. Didn't let them play; and
☐ Let the game get out of control.

Striking a balance between these two extremes is by no means an easy task. Basketball, the city game, presents a number of challenges to its referees. The failure to meet any one of them could, and has, resulted in severe legal consequences.

The degree of judgment necessary to master the fine art of knowing when to blow the whistle, the close proximity of the spectators to the playing area, and the sometimes violent nature of body contact between players wearing virtually no protective equipment all combine to make basketball one of the most difficult sports to officiate.

Top basketball officials have a tremendous ability to handle people while inspiring confidence at the same time. The extent to which you can cultivate this ability, coupled with the observing of a few simple precautions following the guidelines set forth in the rule and case books, can diminish your chances of incurring legal liability for an injury occurring during a basketball game.

Let's get down to brass tacks. As usual, one of our first concerns is for facilities and equipment. There isn't too much you can do about a court that doubles as a parish house auditorium, with a stage as the end line; or lighting so dim that it makes you wish you had one of those helmets that coal miners wear to guide you up and down the floor.

You should at least be aware, however, that the rules require padding on backboards covering the bottom surface of the board and 15 inches up on each side. This padding material is supposed to be at least 2 inches thick and the front surface of the backboard must be covered to a minimum distance of ¾" from the front edge. Fortunately, for most of the games involving players who can get high enough in the air to make contact with any part of the backboard, the level of competition will be such that the equipment is first rate and in conformity with the rules. You may find yourself in a situation, though, where you are working independent ball with college age or older players in a less than adequate facility. If this is the case, I'm not suggesting that you take off your whistle and go home if the backboard isn't properly padded, but if you choose to play the game, be aware that in the event of an injury, no matter how unlikely it may seem, you may hear from someone in the form of a lawsuit.

Player equipment is seldom a problem in basketball, simply because, as a rule, there isn't any. However, when protective equipment is worn, beware of what is and is not permitted by the rules and the type of judgments you may have to make. The rule book regarding equipment is almost identical for the National High School Federation and NCAA College. The key is that rule 3-4-5 in both books begins with the statement that:

> The referee shall not permit any player to wear equipment that, in his judgment, is dangerous to other players.

The rules state that the following materials, when used on elbow, hand, finger, wrist or forearm, are illegal: leather (National Federation says "hard and unyielding leather," plaster, pliable (soft) plaster, metal or any other hard substance, even though covered with soft padding.

Headwear and decorations are illegal. Jewelry is illegal. Headbands may be worn provided they are no wider than 2 inches and made of non-abrasive, unadorned, one-color material, either cloth, elastic, fiber, soft leather, pliable plastic or rubber. The National Federation specifies that rubber bands may be used to control hair. Both codes state that any equipment which unnaturally increases a player's height or reach or aids a player in gaining an advantage is not permitted.

The key here is taking note of any protective equipment or accoutrements and determining whether or not the equipment is on the list of prohibited items, and if it is not on the list of prohibited items, is a danger presented to other players by the use of this equipment? If the answer to either of these two questions is yes, then the player should not be permitted to participate until he removes the equipment.

The two items that had given officials some trouble in the past were the knee brace and various forms of protective devices to assist the player playing with a broken nose. The knee brace problem has been resolved by case book statements indicating that a properly covered "traditional basketball knee brace" may be worn.

With respect to protective devices for a broken nose, the rules say that such a device is permissible if it is not sharp and has no cutting edge nor extends so as to endanger other players. This will have to be judged on a case by case basis. Remember, the important thing is that the referee make a common sense decision so later on, even in the event of a freak injury involving the device, the explanation given will lead one to the conclusion that the referee's decision was a *reasonable* decision under all the facts and circumstances.

ITEMS WORN BY PLAYERS

You will of course want to inspect the 10 starters casually as they make their way onto the floor, for any signs of jewelry or other articles which are not part of the basketball uniform and which may not be worn. Of course, no jewelry of any type is permissible, and it is your job as the official to disallow participation by any player wearing jewelry. Nor may you allow a player to wear head decorations other than the plain headband specified in the rules. Particularly in girls' basketball, the plastic hairpin, the metal barrette and related items can be a problem. The High School Federation provides that only rubber bands are acceptable to control hair. Certain other rules used for womens' basketball permit certain types of hair control devices to be worn.

If you are playing under a set of rules that permits hairpins, barrettes and the like, be sure that the rule is complied with fully and strictly, and if you entertain any doubt that the barrette or whatever conforms to the rule, I would strongly advise you to disallow its use and suggest that it be replaced with rubber bands. The reason is simple; if the hairpin, "legal" according to the rules, should either fall off or come into contact with an opponent in such a way that the opponent is injured, there is a strong possibility that you could be sued for failing to exercise reasonable judgment in inspecting equipment and allowing for its use under conditions calculated to minimize the chance of injury. If the hairpin is loose enough to fall off or had a sharp enough edge or surface that it was able to injure somebody, it could be a freakish type accident. However, you still may well be the one on the hook. Unless these rules are cleaned up and various splinter groups bring their thinking into line with a realistic and sensible approach to preventing injuries, we as officials have the most to lose.

Once the game starts, if perspiration, or a leaky roof makes the playing surface slippery, be aware of the condition. Ideally, the home team or the administration should have a custodian or student manager available to handle mopping up floors when necessary. This is preferable by far to you doing any clean-up work yourself. Let someone else do it. It may not be always possible to get someone else, but remember, if you mop up, you had better do it thoroughly or someone may claim that you negligently handled even this job, thereby causing him to slip and sustain an injury.

Also, as one of my astute basketball official friends used to say, if you use the towel, someone will undoubtedly announce that you are better suited to mopping floors than officiating!

INJURIES

Basketball rules have an unusual (as compared to other sports) provision with respect to stopping play in the event of an injury. This provision is shared neither by baseball nor by football. It's well worth looking into. Rule 5-8-4 concludes that:

> When necessary to protect an injured player, the official may suspend play immediately.

As basketall officials know, under normal circumstances the official is permitted to suspend play when the ball is dead or in control of the injured player's team, or when the opponents complete a play, either by losing control or holding the ball. However, in basketball the play may be suspended at any time if necessary to protect an injured player. You should know this in the event you have to defend your actions in not suspending play when a player is injured. Therefore, if a player appears to you to be injured, you must do some very quick thinking. This should not present too much of a problem: basketball is a fast moving, fast action sport. It requires decisive and quick thinking officials to properly administer all aspects of the game.

In case of an injury, quick thinking by an official can be extremely important. When you have an injury and the ball is alive, ask yourself immediately: "Who's got the ball?" If the answer is the opponent of the injured player, ask yourself, again quickly: "Will this player stand a chance of being further injured if I don't blow the whistle *now?*" If you are convinced that play could go forward and the injured player is not bleeding profusely, unconscious, nor in danger of being trampled to death, you may make a reasonable judgment that you will permit the opponents to complete a play. Then, once this has happened, immediately sound a whistle.

But, at this point you are still not finished dealing with the injury. Since the rules provide that a time-out need not be charged to an injured player's team if the injured player is immediately ready to play, it is your responsibility to inquire of the injured player if he is indeed ready to play immediately. If the answer is yes, play. If the answer is anything other than a definite and convincing yes, beckon the coach and/or trainer onto the floor to attend to the injury.

Remember this: once you beckon bench personnel to come onto the floor, the injured player must be replaced until the next opportunity to substitute after the clock has started following his replacement, or his team will be charged with a time-out for each minute or fraction of a minute consumed in this period.

If, on the other hand, the player is immobile and requires attention on the floor, be sure that you inform the coach and/or trainer that it is not necessary to rush, nor is it necessary to move the player from the court until medical personnel makes the determination that they are able to do so safely. There is of course no penalty, since the player is going to be substituted for, and, you will never want to be accused of urging the removal of the player to get the game moving. Never attempt this.

GAME CONTROL

Ten fast moving, agile bodies confined to a limited area, are bound to collide with each other once in a while. As I said to you at the beginning of the book, you are not reading an Officials' Manual. Heaven knows, there are scores of individuals much better suited than I to tell you how to officiate a basketball game. Your own good judgment (yes, that elusive quality of judgment), common sense and a basic feel for the game will be of tremendous value to you in your career as a basketball official and in minimizing your exposure to a lawsuit.

As we all know, much of the time injuries resulting from rough play are things that we can do little about. It's extremely fashionable to place the blame on the referees by calmly and confidently stating "the officials let the game get out of control."

The type of game that usually preceeds such a remark is a game not that the officials "let get out of control" but a game in which 10 players decided that they did not want to play, but rather to grab, elbow, take poor shots, and look for alibis. Or, how about the game that the official "let get out of control" where one team, with a 20-point lead and 30 seconds to go, calls a time-out after each basket scored by the opponent in that last 30-second period? When one team is pushed into a corner, and the inevitable results, how easy is it to point a finger of blame at the striped shirts?

But, it's an officiating fact of life that, when something goes wrong, we must be prepared to defend our actions if necessary.

Of course, the one area in which officials collectively must legitimately take the blame for violence that may arise either on the court or even to the extent that spectators become involved is that of bench conduct. It's been said that there is virtually no instance of crowd violence on record during or after a basketball game in which there was not some coach-official conflict preceeding the incident.

Over the years, about as many different solutions have been devised as there are leagues and conferences, all revolving around the infamous rule 10-10. Some state high school athletic associations have implemented coaching rules that are more restrictive than that contained in the rule book. For example, a few years ago, the Pennsylvania Interscholastic Athletic Association circulated a memorandum to all officials and member school principals. The memo told of the concern that

. . . the basketball programs throughout the P.I.A.A. are not impaired by the actions of a relatively small group of adult fans, adults who pose a "crowd-control" problem throughout the entire nation. Basketball, as in no other sport, requires the coach to exercise enormous influence over the actions and reactions of the adult fan. Coaching gestures are many times misunderstood by fans and create crowd-control problems . . .

When a coach is ejected from the game, it is his/her responsibility to leave the gymnasium at once. Leaving the gymnasium means physically removing oneself from the area; not sitting in the stands and not remaining in the doorway.

If the ejection of a coach leaves a team without adult supervision as approved by the principal, the game shall be forfeited. Officials are required to report each technical call on a coach or other non-uniformed personnel; and shall also report whenever a player is ejected for other than five (5) personal fouls. P.I.A.A. Basketball Chapter by the P.I.A.A. office. Following the receipt of technical foul reports, the P.I.A.A. distributes copies to each school's principal involved, each P.I.A.A. District Chairman, with another copy in the school's permanent record.

Of all P.I.A.A. activities, basketball is, by far, the most widely contested program. For that reason alone, basketball has the potential for the most abuses of crowd control. P.I.A.A. Restrictive Coaching Rule is an integral part of the total crowd control program at any basketball game and it is to be enforced indiscriminately at all levels of boys and girls basketball from junior high to JV, through senior high varsity contests (emphasis supplied).

The conflict, of course, is between the rules makers seeking to promulgate certain standards of bench conduct and the cadre of coaches who, for various reasons, insist on coaching the game on their feet. According to former P.I.A.A. Executive Director I. Charles McCullough, officials in Pennsylvania have been suspended from the association for failing to enforce the bench conduct rule as written. This procedure, however, has been the exception rather than the rule.

Despite the myriad of restrictive coaching rules and devices written into the rules and regulations of various conferences indicating when a coach may and may not leave his seat on the bench, or otherwise make his presence known, all have proved a failure. Why? Probably because the sport has always been played with coaches at some levels waltzing up and down the sidelines, and, too, the sport has always been played with a divided camp of officials. The rules makers in good faith had attempted, by these various written rules, to take the judgment out of the officiating process as far as bench conduct goes, by making the decision a mechanical one. This is fine as long as coaches can have an expectation of consistency on our part. However, as we know, in very few lead states or conferences has this consistency been forthcoming.

So, determining whether to penalize a coach under the bench conduct rule remains one of the most severe tests of an official's judgment. It's a tall order to both maintain your authority during a hotly contested game and also adopt an empathetic attitude toward coaches who may have a lot riding on the outcome of the game. Of course, even officials are human, and we all have a different level of tolerance and a somewhat individualized conception of the acceptable and the non-acceptable in terms of bench conduct. In reacting to the pressure of screaming coaches and an unruly crowd, the veteran official will always have an edge over an inexperienced official. The veteran official knows that many times a coach will purposely seek to draw a technical foul to either inspire his team to a more intense performance, or to "set the official up," hoping that a weak official will direct his next call in favor of the ranting and raving coach. The veteran official also knows that the motivation for the coach's behavior is not always so important as the effect this behavior has on the players, the other coach and the crowd.

Let me again caution you: This book is not an officiating manual, as I told you. I am the last one to tell you how to officiate. But, if your integrity is being questioned within earshot of others or an episode of name-calling occurs, again, under circumstances that others hear what is going on, if you do not penalize in these two instances, you may be hard pressed to justify your actions should an assault upon you occur during or after the game.

For one of the first questions that somebody always asks at a league or conference disciplinary hearing when misconduct towards an official has been charged is, did you, Mr. Referee, penalize the coach or the player during the game for remarks or actions that preceded the alleged assault? If your answer is no, the league or review committee may well conclude that you, the official, precipitated the action against you. An unjust result? Sure. Unfortunately, it's the way things work. Remember that Heaven, and commissioners, help those who help themselves.

Incidentally, the colleges and the High School Federation have cleaned up bench conduct quite a bit by placing a provision in rule 10-10 charging the head coach with a technical foul if any bench personnel are charged with a technical foul. Thus, the days of the head coach sending a sacrificial lamb to the altar to do his dirty work are virtually eliminated. For, if an assistant coach, a trainer, and a substitute each are charged with one technical, the head coach is ejected!

In some states, also, state high school associations require that, if there is only one coach or adult supervisor present with a team, as frequently happens on the underclass level, that coach may not be ejected under the rules of basketball, but rather, under circumstances where his ejection is mandated, he is to remain in the bleachers so that he can still supervise his team. Other states provide that in the event of an ejection of the sole faculty member travelling with the team, the game is forfeited.

Obviously, the latter provision is far superior. The idea of putting the onus on the official for doing his job by enforcing bench conduct, has many legal implications for the official, all of them bad.

For, by placing the coach in the bleachers, he is in a legal never-never land. He is supposed to be available, in case there is an injury or some other difficulty, to attend to his team, yet it is the official who has placed him out of contact with his team and therefore less able to render assistance.

Therefore, if there is one change which you should, right now, lobby to have made, it is this: the adoption of the "Pennsylvania Rule" wherein if there is no faculty member to supervise a team and in the event of an ejection of the sole coach, the game is over. Not only does this limit your chances for liability for injuries to players, but also it eliminates the specter of an unruly coach, whose conduct is already outrageous, to spread the gospel to every misfit seated in the bleachers and thereby cause a potential danger to you and your partner. Hopefully, too, if underclass coaches know that they will have some explaining to do after a forfeit of an underclass game, their behavior might improve.

As to players on the court, I can't tell you what to do. But listen to what Dave Tobey,one of the great basketball referees around these parts in the 1940s, said in his book, entitled *Basketball Officiating:*

> Of course, now and then a boy will act up, especially on his 4th [in 1943 it took only 4], or disqualifying foul. But if he doesn't get abusive, do not penalize him. You must distinguish between ill temper directed at you, which must be called, and actions which indicate the player is just annoyed at himself. If this burst of temperament is intended to arouse the sympathy of the crowd or the coach, quickly call a technical foul.

By the way, if you ever come across a copy of *Basketball Officiating* by Dave Tobey, grab it. The mechanics and some of the rules discussions are, of course, outdated; the photographs are a scream; but much of the text is extremely worthwhile reading for any basketball official. For example, Tobey offers these guidelines as to contacts between players:

> If you cannot distinguish between meaningless nudges that do no harm and the slightest push that does damage, you will never become a good official. Learn to recognize favorable and unfavorable positions of the players when contact occurs. Unavoidable contacts from favorable positions are not fouls. Unfortunately,

Officials can and in fact have been sued for allegedly not calling enough fouls with the result that an injury occurred which was then sought to be blamed upon the officials.

there are officials who are not happy, and do not feel they have earned their fees, unless they call 40 or 50 fouls a game.

At least, you know you'll never be sued for not calling enough fouls, right? Wrong! Yes, Virginia, officials can and in fact have been sued for allegedly not calling enough fouls with the result that an injury occurred which was then sought to be blamed upon the officials.

Consider the case of the two basketball officials working a high school contest in the state of Washington in the early 1970s.[1]

A foul occurred with 1:06 remaining in the game. The young man who was fouled apparently was catapulted over his opponent's shoulder and landed on his head in such a way that the cervical vertebrae were fractured and he was rendered a quadraplegic. A lawsuit was brought against, not only both school boards, both coaches and their wives, but both officials, their wives and their Official's Association, in addition to the Washington Interscholastic Athletic Association.

Among other things, the officials were charged in the lawsuit with negligence for failing to call fouls during rough play or terminate the game, thus proximately causing the injury. Fortunately, films of the game were available and, according to one of the attorneys, they depicted the plaintiff jumping into the air and landing on the man with the ball, which at least indicates that plaintiff had some considerable degree of participation in the incident which caused this tragic injury.

Interestingly, one official had no insurance coverage. The other official was fortunate enough to have his Homeowners Insurance policy cover his defense. The referees' association did not maintain insurance.

All the defendants in the case moved the court for summary judgment and their motions were granted. However, the injured basketball player appealed and, while the appeal was pending, the case was settled.

Incidents such as these surely cannot always be avoided. As an official, you can, however, often prevent a fight between players which could lead to nasty legal consequences for you. How's it done? Basically, by doing things that all competent officials do as a matter of course; you keep your head up and you are at all times prepared to move quickly and decisively. In other words, be watching and supervising all 10 players so if a situation develops that appears as if it's going to blossom into fisticuffs, you are able to move between the opponents in such a way that they will see the stripes and realize the nature of the animal whose jungle they have invaded.

I have had officials say to me the they are not policemen and are loath to get in the middle between two angry tree tops. While all of that is well and good, remember that one punch, well placed can be the precipitator of bigger things to come, escalating from a few missing teeth to a full scale riot. If the worst happens, people are going to remark how the officials let the game get away from them and, as we have seen in "The Liability Trap," in the event of a severe injury, a lawsuit may well be brought against officials in the game where a fight occurred.

Often (but not always), players who fight are reacting to a challenge and feel that they must save face by not shrinking from a fight. That's where you come in. If you can get to a point between the opponents fast enough so they can see your uniformed presence, then both combatants are able to save face as the big bad official intervened. No, you can't always get there fast enough, nor are you always going to have your sights set on all 10 players at once.

Indeed, the drastic change in officiating mechanics adopted by the colleges and high schools in 1972, requiring the non-calling official, after a foul, to "freeze" his attention on the players while the other official was reporting the foul (as opposed to the earlier mechanics which had the non-calling official chasing down the basketball after his partner had called a foul), was a direct result of the 1971 college basketball game between the University of Minnesota and Ohio State University, in which one of the ugliest fights in the annals of college basketball occurred, between Minnesota's Corky Taylor and Ron Behagen and Ohio State's Luke Witte. You may recall that there were not 2 but 3 officials working that game. They all were exercising their proper mechanics of the day.

6

CHECK-UP FOR FOOTBALL OFFICIALS

"Go out and hit somebody!!" The tough-nosed football coach, veins bolting from his temples, exhorts his charges at the pregame pep talk. Whether or not the team follows his advice and goes out and hits somebody is the coach's business; how they hit somebody is yours.

If you're going to officiate football in such a way that you minimize your exposure to legal liability, it is impossible for you to "fake it" by arriving 10 minutes before game time. You must be prepared to come early, (although this is one job where you will not be expected to both come early and stay late). This is true no matter how many officials are on the game. At any level of football, you, the official, are required to inspect the field and visit with each team to determine the legality of equipment to be worn by players.

Though both High School Federation and NCAA College rules require the referee to inspect the field before the game, it is common practice for this duty to be delegated to be shared by some or all of the officials on a given crew. The mechanical aspect of the field inspection varies somewhat by area, conference, level of play and size of crew. However, what is important is that the field is inspected by more than one of the 2, 3, 4, 5, or 6 game officials. The inspection of the field is vital for two reasons; the American football field is 120 yards long and almost 55 yards wide (and the Canadian field is larger) and it is a virtual certainty that about every inch of the field will be occupied at one time or another by one or more of the 22 participants.

Not only do you want to inspect the field to assure yourself that there are no obstacles such as exposed drains, broken bottles, exposed sprinkler valves, or foxholes capable of ensnaring even the most agile linebacker, but you will also need to inspect field markings, goal posts and pylons to determine the legality of all of these items. And, you will want to know whether or not you have a completely marked field and that your sidelines, endlines, goal lines, hash marks, and whatever yard lines you have are intact. For example, if the goal line looks as it it were laid down by a groundskeeper who was instead plotting an outline of the inlets along the Gulf of Mexico, you will want to correct this situation, not for safety's sake, but so you may have an even shot at determining whether or not the ball breaks the plane of the goal line. Also, if the field is used for soccer or other sports, there may be extraneous markings and lines of which you will want to be aware and of which you will want to make your partners aware, lest somebody blow a whistle when the ballcarrier crosses a soccer side-line or goal crease.

If, on your inspection, you find foreign objects on the field which could constitute safety hazards, retrieve the groundskeeper or game management and have them removed. Do not attempt to get a shovel and cover the drain pipe or the hole yourself. Instruct that it be done and revisit the site of the problem to make sure that the correction has been done properly. This is your duty.

For many years, the responsibility for determining the legality of equipment worn by players rested with the umpire. To discharge this duty, it was necessary for the umpire to inspect the equipment employed by most teams; a task which, given the size of the typical football squad, was formidable. In actual practice, many umpires, upon visiting the locker room or the bench area before the game, would simply inquire if there was any unusual taping or brace work which should be examined. Although this was not by any means a satisfactory approach, practicalities of the situation often made it difficult for an umpire to inspect the arms, legs, head and torso of 75 to 100 football players in the brief period before game time. Consequently, the High School Federation, over a period of years, has evolved a shift of responsibility, as it were, from the umpire to the head coach as regards player equipment. The 1982 High School Federation Rule Book states that

> Prior to the start of the game, the head coach shall be responsible for verifying to the referee that all of his players are equipped in compliance with these rules. Any question regarding legality of a player's equipment shall be determined by the umpire.

Although widely hailed by officials and interpreters as a breakthrough in simplifying life for the game officials, most notably the umpire, this change does not mean that field officials are absolved from liability in the event that improper or illegal equipment is used during the game. It is definitely a step in the right direction and hopefully other sports will enact similar rules.

In essence, the 1982 rule change, requiring the head coach to verify that all players are legally equipped in accordance with the rules regarding helmets, instituted by the High School Federation in 1980. The 1980 rule required the head coach to verify that all his players were equipped with helmets approved by the National Operating Committee on Standards for Athletic Equipment (NOCSAE). The National Operating Committee on Standards for Athletic Equipment began testing football helmets in 1973. NOCSAE is a joint project of various amateur athletic associations (including the NCAA and the High School Federation), and some athletic equipment trade associations. They say they test the football helmet by placing it on an artificial head and dropping it from a height of 6 feet 16 times. Then, shock measurements are taken to develop a standard called the "Severity Index" for concussion tolerance. The test is said to simulate a fleet-footed football player running at 17.9 feet per second and crashing headlong into a flat surface which stopped his head in less than 1 inch.

Anyway, as with most High School Federation rule changes involving equipment, there was a period when the use of NOCSAE approved helmets was recommended pending the requirement that all players be equipped with the same helmets. In 1980 when the requirement was put into effect regarding helmets, it was said that it was the responsibility of the head coach to verify to the referee that his players were in fact equipped with NOCSAE-approved helmets. The idea being that it was impractical to expect the umpire to inspect the helmets of each squad member for the NOCSAE seal.

In 1982, it was an easy jump to require the head coach to verify a little more information to the referee before game time.

It's interesting to note that when the head coach was first required to verify that his team was equipped with NOCSAE approved helmets, some officials devised a written form to submit to each head coach prior to the game, wherein the coach was requested to put his signature on the bottom line of a document stating that his team was in fact equipped with NOCSAE approved helmets. These forms took a variety of shapes and sizes, but all had one thing in common; they don't work. The use of such forms is a textbook example of officials getting involved in an area beyond their proper mechanics and procedures, which can only have a negative effect if there are any claims later made against them.

This is so for several reasons. Firstly, a form that is not professionally drafted may have the opposite effect, i.e., that of shifting liability back to the official by virtue of the official's negligence in failing to ascertain the required information from the coach. More importantly, handing a head coach, responsible for pleasing an athletic director, a stadium, full of parents and others whose taxes pay his salary, and a squad of 50 high-strung and unpredictable adolescents is tantamount to waving a red flag at a bull 10 minutes before game time. Thirdly, many problems may arise as to the authenticity of the signature, even if the form is worded properly. All in all, the use of unauthorized documents superimposed upon what should be a simple procedure is strongly discouraged.

On the other hand, make sure that you do not forget to ask the magic question, if you're the referee, when you go to meet each head coach. First of all, needless to say, make sure that you're talking to the head coach and, *in the presence of the umpire* and other officials, if possible, ask the coach this question: "Coach, are all your players equipped in compliance with the rules?" If the answer is *anything* other that yes, find out why and have the umpire examine whatever it was that caused the head coach to hesitate or equivocate in his answer. Remember, the umpire must be satisfied that the equipment is legal according to the rules. This is not the time to be a "nice guy" and overlook any other requirements.

The 1982 High School Federation rules require, in addition to a NOCSAE certified helmet, a face protector, a mouth and tooth protector which protects and separates the biting surfaces and protects the lips, soft knee pads worn over the knees and covered by the pants at least one-half inch thick, or, if made of an approved shock absorbent material, three-eighths of an inch thick; hip pads, shoulder pads fully covered by a jersey; thigh guards; and shoes.

Illegal equipment, according to the High School Federation code is equipment which, "*in the opinion of the umpire*, (emphasis supplied) is dangerous or confusing." The rules go on to specify that illegal equipment includes but is not limited to:

- projecting metal or other hard substance on clothes or person;
- knee, elbow, hand, wrist, or forearm guard or brace made of sole leather, plaster, metal or other hard substance in its final form, and even though covered with soft padding;
- knee braces made of hard unyielding material, unless hinges are covered on both sides and all of its edges overlapped, and any other hard substance is covered with at least 1/2 inch of closed-cell slow recovery rubber or other material of the same minimum thickness and having similar physical properties;
- forearm pads, hand pads or gloves, unless sanctioned by the umpire as being made entirely of soft non-abrasive, non-hardening material, athletic tape may be used at each end to anchor such pads;
- tape or bandage on the hand or forearm, unless sanctioned by the umpire as being nonabrasive and necessary to protect an existing injury. Non-hardening, non-abrasive tape or bandage (not to exceed 3 thicknesses) and sweatbands, when any of these are worn on the wrist beginning at the base of the thumb (proximal end of the metacarpal bone) and extending not more than 3 inches toward the elbow, are legal, without inspection or sanction;

- shin or thigh guards of any hard substance, unless the outside surface and all edges are covered with soft material at least 1/2 inch thick or 3/8 inch thick if made of an approved shock-absorbing material;
  NOTE: For new equipment, the Rules Committee strongly recommends these requirements also apply to hip, rib, and shoulder pads.
- shoes which do not meet the following specifications are illegal: the shoe shall be made of a material which covers the foot (canvas, leather or synthetic) attached to a firm sole of leather, rubber, or composition material which may have cleats, which comply with specifications listed in item (h) below, or which may be cleatless. Among the items which do not meet these requirements are gymnastic slippers, tennis shoes cut so protection is reduced, ski and logger boots, and other apparel not intended for football use.

This section goes on to describe the details of measurements for shoe cleats, with the proviso that cleats, studs or projections which are 1/2 inch or less in length and made of rubber or rubber type synthetic material that is not abrasive and does not cut are legal.

If you are a college official, you know that the list of required equipment is similar to High School Federation, with the exception that the NCAA does not require players to wear shoes.

While the High School Federation provides a penalty against the coach for unsportsmanlike conduct, the NCAA code does not provide any specific penalty for wearing illegal equipment. The point is, if you're playing High School Federation rules, in the event of illegal equipment, be sure to enforce the prescribed penalties. And, you should be alert as a reasonable official to the possibility that illegal equipment will find its way on to the field. If it's there you must deal with it.

This means, if you do get the unusually troublesome coach, who repeats the violation for failure to wear required equipment continuously, you must, on a subsequent offense, penalize him 15 yards and charge the coach individually with an unsportsmanlike foul which counts toward his total permissible unsportsmanlike fouls of two for disqualification.

PREGAME DUTIES OF THE LINESMAN

During a National Football League preseason game in 1972, all-pro defensive end Charles "Bubba" Smith was at his post when a teammate intercepted a pass. At the end of the play, Mr. Smith found himself on the ground, out of bounds, and suffering from a serious knee injury. A lawsuit was brought against several parties, including the NFL head linesman, Ed Marion, and the individual who was holding the down marker which Smith allegedly collided with upon going out of bounds.

The first trial of the case resulted in a mistrial due to the fact that the jurors could not agree on a unanimous verdict. The second trial of the case resulted in a ruling in favor of the defendants. Of course, the NFL official was able to testify that he had instructed the chain crew in the proper methods of holding the stakes or the outcome may have been quite different.

Don't think it can happen to you? Guess again. If a National Football League game, with all the attention paid to officiating, with seven game officials working and with a competent and enthusiastic down marker crew, could result in the linesman even having to defend the suit for injuries occurring during that game, think of the trouble us little folk on the club, Pop Warner, and even college level could get into.

How many times, even at varsity high school games, have you had to send coaches and athletic directors scouring the stands to find someone who would graciously consent to hold the chains? How many times have you gone to an underclass game and had to literally drag people off the sidelines to perform the task?

How many times have you been faced with indifferent, uncooperative or just plain inept persons who are barely interested in watching the game, no less being part of an officiating team? How many times have you been handed three young grammar school age youngsters to hold the two 7 foot aluminum rods and 10 yards of chain that could cripple the player for life?

Even under the best of circumstances, with competent and knowledgeable adults, there is simply no excuse for failing to take the time to properly instruct these people before the opening kick-off. This is so vital that the start of the game should and must be delayed if this instruction has not been given. This is clearly not the time for a lick and a promise. Certainly a little bit of psychology is necessary here. Once you have the personnel, common sense dictates a name to name introduction with each of the crew members. Ideally, there will be four persons assigned to you. You may have to get by with three. If that's the case, instructions are all the more important. If you're a leader of men (or women) now's the time to show it. If you are able to get across to these people on your chain crew that their alert attention to what you are saying could mean the difference between not only a well-officiated game and a sloppy mess, but also the difference between a player remaining intact and a player praying for his life, you will have gone a long way toward having minimized your legal exposure.

At this time, both High School Federation and NCAA College Rules specify that the down marker equipment shall be operated outside, and not on, the sidelines. You will want to pay attention to this rule and also you will want to instruct these individuals, in addition to their general procedure, that if the play develops toward their sideline, not to lift the chains but rather to drop them down and straight back. Also, it is important that these people be told that they are not at any time to leave the poles unattended, not between plays, not during time outs, not at any time; that they must have their hands on them at all times.

In High School Federation football, we know that the jurisdiction of the officials begins 30 minutes before game time.

The practicalities of arrival at the game site, finding a place to park, getting into the dressing room, finding the teams' locker room and assorted other items of debris in the high, muddy waters of starting a football game make it sometimes impossible for officials to be out on the football field one half hour before game time to watch for unsportsmanlike actions by either team. But, remember this: if you do have a major incident wherein someone is injured 29 minutes before game time, you may have a problem. Therefore, be conscious of the rule and try to have at least two members of the crew make their presence known to both teams one-half hour before game time.

A rule which was placed in the High School Federation Rule Book several years ago specifies that during the coin toss all squad personnel other than the captains shall remain in the team box vicinity. This would seem to preclude players such as this year's graduating seniors or a disabled honorary co-captain who is unable to suit up from going out to the hash mark or otherwise participating in the coin toss ceremony. Here again, the story goes that several years back teams lined up on the hash mark during the coin toss and proceeded to hurl insults at each other, resulting in a near riot. That's why the rule is written as it is; that's the foreseeable consequence of not following the rule, therefore follow the rule. Don't be a nice guy and let the team stray from the team box because if something untoward happens you are at fault.

At the toss of the coin, if your position is other than referee, remember that you are out in the middle of the field for very good reason other than just to be introduced to the captains (who don't care who you are anyway). It is important that each and every official witness the coin toss and record the results of that coin toss.

Now, let's get the game started. If you're one of the "wing" officials, remember to keep your sidelines clear. The 2-yard area between the sideline and the restraining line in the team box is designed so that someone is able to use that area in which to work, and that someone is you, the linesman or line judge. Don't let coaches, players, photographers and statisticians occupy the area that you need to work in. Just don't permit it. If you do, when you have an out of bounds play, you're going to have a great deal of trouble finding a spot and determining who's a player and who isn't. Also, someone over there could get hurt and try to place the blame on you.

Similarly, between the 30-yard lines and the respective end of the field, don't permit statisticians, photographers and spectators to stand any closer than you permit coaches and players to stand in the team box. Keep everyone back, and if necessary enlist the aid of police or other security personnel on the site. If it's necessary to delay the game to do so, do it. For none of these people will necessarily spare you if they file a lawsuit should they be run over by a barrelling football player. Again, although an injured person may not, and probably would not, win such a lawsuit, why be in the position of having to defend it and having your name associated with it. Don't let others place you in a position where you could get in trouble. Every time you put on the striped shirt you're in the position where you could get in trouble, so don't let others increase your exposure when you can do something about it!

Once the game starts, know well what the rules permit opponents to do to each other in terms of person-to-person contact.

Similarly, when the ballcarrier is driven out of bound by an opponent, remember that one or more of the ball players is going to be on the other team's sideline and a tackle that's a little bit "too hard," or a ballcarrier who struggles aggressively to get away from his tackler may provoke a response from one or the other's teammates along the sideline. Therefore, if you are working a 4 person or even a 3 person crew, take the advice of the Officials' Manual: Drop your bean bag at the out of bounds spot, continue to observe play, and, if you have no backup official with you, go to the opponents out of bounds. MAKE THEM SEE THE STRIPED SHIRT BETWEEN THEMSELVES AND THEIR OPPONENTS. This can prevent a bad scene. Ideally, if you are working with 4, 5 or 6 officials, you will have a backup official to take the opponents out of bounds and one to get the spot. If you are working with less than 4 officials, or even in a 4 man game, this may not always be possible. Therefore, the covering official must be vigilant enough to handle an out of bounds situation without help until help arrives.

Every time you put on the striped shirt you're in the position where you could get in trouble.

INJURIES

Although injuries can and do occur, and there is no known method of absolutely preventing all injuries sustained during athletic competition, what is often as important to our protection as officials as our good mechanics in preventing injuries is the specific mechanics to be used in the event that a player is injured.

There is a specific set of guidelines that must be followed if you are to be successful in minimizing your legal exposure, which, of course, means acting as a reasonably prudent referee, as we have said. Remember this: if a player is injured during the course of play, he may do one of two things: walk off the field under his own power, or remain stationary in prone position or otherwise, awaiting assistance. Which of these two avenues he takes will govern your actions. What Mr. Trainer and Mr. Physician do for the player off the field is their business. What any or all of these people, in addition to team attendants, do with an injured player who becomes immobile on the field is at least partly your business.

This is so because you, the referee, have control of what takes place on the field and when, to the extent that play is started, interrupted, and again resumed.

Therefore, do not place yourself in a position of failing to stop play or resuming play too soon before an injury has been properly dealt with.

The football rules used to give a very nice analysis of the differing penalty enforcements when a foul occurred in or about the time of a score, meaning a try for point or a touchdown. There was a chart set up that showed you 4 separate time periods, and all fouls could be characterized in one of these classifications when they involved a scoring play. This was something like a foul during a down in which a touchdown was scored. That was No. 1. No. 2 was a foul during the dead ball following the successful score and prior to the next time the ball becomes alive. No. 3 was a foul during the try for point. And No. 4 was a foul after the ball becomes dead on the try for point and prior to the ball becoming alive on the ensuing kick-off.

In much the same fashion, we can functionally divide the intervals surrounding the occurrence of an injury to a player into 4 time categories.

The first of these categories is, obviously, the events leading up to the injury and your cognizance of the fact that a player is disabled.

If a player is injured during a live ball, it is impossible to stop play prior to the ball becoming dead by rule. Any such attempt would of course be an inadvertent whistle and would more than likely deprive someone of something. In a fast moving sport such as football played in such a wide area, it is unlikely that an injury will be sufficiently severe to attract much attention prior to the play being over, in any event.

It is of course important that you do not permit players to indiscriminately get into the habit of pouncing on fallen opponents. Nor is it a good practice to pretend that there are no out of bounds lines and look the other way if a player violates a rule governing player conduct and roughness. Warnings do little good in these areas.

If there is a borderline violation, opinions differ widely on how to handle this. A borderline encroachment does no one any harm and may in fact disturb the tempo of an otherwise good game. A borderline forearm in the gut may indeed provoke a fight, a serious injury, or worse in terms of your legal exposure. It is legal death for an official to say "Next time, son, that late hit will be penalized." Mistake one is not penalizing the late hit. Mistake two is telling everyone about it. Veteran officials know this. If you can't make this distinction, you're not doing your job as an official.

The second interval is after the injury occurs, and includes the time up to and including the time the player is removed from the field of play to his penultimate destination. This is a crucial period for the official. First and foremost: *Do not, do not* attempt to treat or manipulate the injured player yourself. You may be a noted physician, you may be a registered nurse, you may even have certificates 8 ways to Sunday in CPR training. If you attempt to render treatment, you may well find yourself facing a lawsuit alleging that you lacked the proper qualifications, equipment and facilities, or otherwise negligently aggravated whatever injuries the player had. Moreover, your job, that day, regardless of your training in other areas, is as an official. Let your conscience be your guide. If you do undertake to use whatever skill or knowledge you have, you are injecting yourself in a situation and must be prepared to suffer the consequences. Although this may sound heartless at first blush, please remember that when all the smoke clears and the injured player begins looking for people to bear his loss, the fellow with the striped shirt who tried to do his best is a very likely target, and it's not likely that anyone is going to have any heart where you're concerned.

Secondly, do not permit teammates to drag an injured player off the field in an effort to get off the next play. At such time as the ambulance crew, coach, trainer, doctor or whatever arrive on the scene, assure the person in charge, preferably in the hearing of others, not to be in a hurry in his treatment or procedures. Assure him that you will wait as long as necessary and that time is not a factor. The invention of the orthopaedic stretcher has done wonders for the art of not further injuring one by moving him impropitiously.

The third interval is after the play is resumed. Do not discuss with anyone your version of the play on which the injury occurred. Nor ought you to use the incident as a vehicle to issue warning to players that in the future such rough play will not be tolerated. Your position is simply that you and the players and the coaches know the rules, and that you enforce the rules from beginning to end.

The fourth of our intervals is after the game. Do not discuss the incident or the injuries with anyone, including the media. Remember, you are there as official, and an official only, not Howard Cosell!

There are certain times during the game when you must become sensitive to the possibility that a dispute between opponents may arise. Since football players are taught in the ways of manly arts, often such a dispute is likely to be resolved by a physical display rather than by the relative niceties of conversation. It often happens that a fight or skirmish will break out when a team feels it has been embarrassed, or worse, humiliated, by its opponents, or when someone feels he is being taken advantage of and reacts to that situation out of frustration, anger and desperation.

In any event, if there's a fight, nobody's going to want to know why it wasn't your fault. You're wearing the striped shirt, you don't let the game get, as they say, out of control. It's as simple as that. Are we saying that if a fight breaks out that it's the officials who always could have prevented it? Of course not, and don't let anybody tell you different. There are some days when tempers are such and when the moods of the participants are such, and when the chemistry, as the commercial says, is just right, that there is nothing anyone, and I mean anyone, can do.

However, we often are forced to eat a stew that we let simmer too long. The Officials' Manual says "anticipate ill will brewing." This is one bromide you should swallow whole.

How do you do this? It's relatively simple. Keep your head up and your eyes open to watch the interaction of the opponents, especially when one team is suffering at the hands of the other. That is to say, after a score, after a particularly hard hit, after an out of bounds play when non-players are involved, after a fumble recovery or an interception, and between quarters when players are milling about, uncertain of exactly where to go and not huddled in the bosoms of their teammates.

Let's take them one at a time:

After a score

When a touchdown is scored, I'll guarantee you one thing. You're going to have at least 11 happy young players and at least 11 equally unhappy opponents. If it's a goal line plunge, according to the defense, the player with the ball was always stopped short, two yards short of the goal line. In any event, after the pile-up and the cooldown, four officials don't have a hell of a lot to do and should not be all that concerned with chasing the ball. It will come back. The covering official may in good time get the ball after he sees all players untangle and everyone on his way to his respective bench.

After a try for a point

Similarly, after a try for a point, there's fertile ground for a fight to break out. Don't stand around with your head down or be busy running upfield to take your position for kick-off.

After a touchdown or after a try for point when the teams are changing large numbers of personnel, this is the time when you have opponents mingling together, unpiling and setting off in different direction to their respective benches. It's a simple matter for one or two officials to track down the ball, and usually after a kick someone will do this for you (your best bet is to commission the ball boy to do this), and toss it back in your direction. In the meanwhile, your spare energies should be taken up not with eyeing the cheerleaders or chatting with your compatriots, but rather with keeping your head up, alert, and watching the players repair to their respective benches. If you are there, your eyes are felt, and, if your eyes are on the field and the opponents, you will be in a position to nip any potential flare-ups in the bud.

Between quarters

Similarly, between quarters, the traditional manuals on officiating indicate that all officials should check the down and distance and the yard line where the ball rests. Although this is true, there is a definite procedure to follow between quarters which, I suggest to you, again has the effect of preventive officiating at its best. The key to it is this. In a 4-man game, at the end of the quarter, the linesman must attend to his chain crew, see to it that the 5-yard line is clipped, and reposition the chains at the appropriate spot. The 3 remaining officials must note where they're going to place the ball in a precise fashion. This is, of course, fundamental. However, while the referee and umpire are preparing to move the ball to its exact location by footsteps or how-ever they do it, the field judge should assume the responsibility of moving to the other end of the field with the 22 football players. Why? As soon as the end of the quarter is announced, the players trudge off to some undetermined location at the other end of the field. They never know where, but they go. When was the last time you ever noticed players on their own accord, left to their own devices, posi-tioning themselves anywhere near the proper yardline for the start of the 2nd or 4th quarter?

At any rate, the real point is that you have 22 opponents all walk-ing away from 4 or 5 officials. Unsupervised. This should never happen. All players must be in view of one or more of the officials at all times. If the ball is on the 12-yard line and a fight breaks out with 22 players 60 yards from 4 officials, this is evidence of poor officiating. It's a simple matter for the field judge to quickly note the down and distance and yard line on his game card and accompany the two teams to the other end of the field. This will not only aid the referee and umpire in coming to the appropriate hash mark and yard line to reset the ball and the stakes, but will aid the teams if you stand where the ball is going to be placed. They'll know where they must set up. But most importantly, all 22 players will be under the supervision of the field judge at all times between periods. Don't let them go alone.

7

CHECK-UP FOR SOCCER OFFICIALS

Maracana Stadium in Brazil holds 220,000. Tear gas toting police sometimes have their hands full protecting soccer referees at Maracana Stadium. However, they are aided by a secret weapon: there's a moat, 15 feet deep and 25 feet wide, that separates the playing field from the stands!

In this country, the meteoric rise in the popularity of the game of soccer on the scholastic level and below has witnessed soccer being played virtually everywhere. Often banished from "Big Town High School's" elegantly manicured football field to the municipal or county park, soccer officials in America often don't even have a rope or a fence separating them from the crowd, let alone a moat!

Fortunately, both NCAA College and National Federation High School Rules require—and you should, too—that spectators be kept a distance of at least 10 feet from the playing field. The NCAA recommends that a physical barrier such as a fence or roping be used to denote this area, while the High School Federation simply pleads that a dash-line mark the area beyond which spectators ought not to venture. Anyone who has officiated for any length of time, (or anyone who has driven an automobile) knows that a painted line seldom restrains anyone from going where he or she is not supposed to be. Therefore, unless you're on a proper field, one with the proper fencing or barriers to separate those who belong and those who are there to watch, you had better be prepared for a rather intimate relationship with the supporters of both teams.

In the event of a throw-in or a corner kick, if you have permitted the spectators to wander near the touch-lines, now is the time when you had better request the athletic director or administering authority to move spectators back. Don't permit a corner kick or a throw-in to be made by a player in the midst of a swarm of spectators. In that circumstance, only bad things can happen.

You should, of course, enlist the aid of any supervisory personnel from the host institution who have been assigned to the game. Often you will not get this kind of cooperation, and that, of course, will make your job more difficult. It will be to your distinct advantage, however, to do your best to keep spectators away from the touch-lines and the goal lines.) And, "away" in this context, when the rules say 10 feet at a minimum, does not mean a yard or two.

In fact, NCAA rules provide for a photographers' line. This line goes from touch-line to touch-line behind each goal, starting at least 2 yards from the corner flag and widening out to a point that is about 3½ yards behind the actual goal area. If you are working a game played under NCAA rules, be aware that such a line exists.

High School Federation rules require that team areas be 20 yards apart, with the area in the middle designated as the official area which spans 10 yards.

As to the field itself, there are two major areas of concern. These are the goals and the flags. Goal posts are to be 8 yards apart, measured from the inside and joined by a cross-bar which is 8 feet from the ground. These 3 obstacles all must measure not less than 4" in width nor more than 5" in depth. The goals, of course, must have nets, and you would not be remiss if you were to breeze by before the start of the game to check out that everything is in order on either end of the field so far as the goals and the nets are concerned. If, for example, you have omitted this part of your duties and a goal is scored with the ball being propelled at great force, it could shoot out the other end beyond the net and strike an unsuspecting bystander who, in turn, may sue you, claiming that you should have checked the nets. Therefore, check the nets! It'll only take a minute. Besides, that's what you're there for.

Make sure also that the top of the net extends backward parallel to the cross-bar, so the goalkeeper can't get caught. Both High School Federation and College rules indicate that this distance should be approximately 2 feet.

The other area of concern is the corner flags. Both High School Federation and NCAA rules provide that soccer fields be marked in their 4 corners with 5-foot high flagpoles to which are attached 1 x 2 foot flags. The option is also provided to place 2 additional flags directly opposite each other at midfield, at least 1 yard outside the touch-lines. The only safety requirement discernable in the rules is that the top of the flagpost be not pointed. High School Federation rules also specify that the flag itself shall not have a pointed top and that the post shall be of some smooth material. With the rules as they are presently written, there is little you can do about a player being injured by running into a 5-foot rigid stake in pursuit of the soccer ball or an opponent. Some day, hopefully, in the not too distant future, the makers of these devices will heed the latest technology (perhaps inspired by a lawsuit or two) and fashion a collapsible foam pylon, similar to those devised several years ago to replace the old corner flags in use in American football.

Indeed, the NCAA states that for artificial playing surfaces a soft cellulose pylon or a flexible wire coil flag may be used.

In the meanwhile, the best you can do is make sure that the flags and their staffs conform to the existing regulations, i.e., that they are smooth, do not have pointed tops, and are properly placed.

Both NCAA College and High School Federation rules require the referee to examine the equipment of *each player* before the game. Requirements as to equipment vary between the two codes of rules.

The NCAA College Code simply states that "a player shall not wear anything that is dangerous to another player," but added that *hard* protective equipment is also termed illegal.

High School Federation rules are considerably more specific with respect to equipment. In high school competition, any projecting metal or other hard plates, projections on clothing or sole leather, fiber, metal or unyielding materials in the head, arm, thigh or hip pads are illegal. Headwear, face or eyeglass guards, or any type of cast is illegal. Also covered is a prohibition against the wearing of jewelry by players, except that religious or medical metals may be taped inside the uniform.

Shoes must also be inspected before the game. NCAA College and High School Federation rules are similar with respect to the types of footwear allowed. The major difference is that the High School Federation does not permit any aluminum cleats, nor are steel tips on plastic cleats permitted, as they are in college competition.

National Federation rules similarly provide that the referee shall "examine the uniform and equipment of each player to see that it complies with the rules."

The field and players having been inspected by you, the next item of business will be the coin toss. At the toss of the coin, if your position is other than referee, remember that you are out in the middle of the field for very good reason other than just to be introduced to the captains (who don't care who you are anyway). It is important that each official witness the coin toss and record the results of that coin toss. Also, as referee, you *must* indicate to both captains that an intentional foul of the goal keeper in possession of the ball will result in immediate ejection.

And, of course, the team that wins the toss has the choice of end of the field or the kick-off. The loser of the toss has no choice.

As is the case with all of the team sports that we have been discussing, a very real threat to our legal well-being as officials can arise in the area of game control. We have seen how a basketball referee was sued for allegedly failing to call enough fouls to deter a crippling attack against one player by another. We have seen how a wrestling referee was taken to task in the courts by supposedly failing to penalize for illegal holds and maneuvers being applied by one opponent against another. We have all heard of the baseball umpire attacked after the game by the very person who he should have had the intelligence and fortitude to eject an hour earlier.

It should be no surprise, then, that today's soccer official, charged with supervising the antics of 22 players and a host of coaches, spectators, administrators and the like in a large outdoor area, needs to be ever alert for the welfare of players who sometimes do collide with one another.

Consequently, it helps to not only know the illegal acts which a player can commit, but also to have a "feel" for the game, and this includes the ability to distinguish various types of contact which may place one team at a disadvantage from that conduct that has no such effect. Coupled with all this is the ability to inspire confidence in the players so they may perform to the best of their capabilities.

There is a remarkable similarity in many areas between the viewpoints of, say, Irv Brown, one of the most highly regarded basketball officials of the recent era, and well known British soccer referee Gordon Hill. Brown always felt that a good basketball official should be visible in that he is constantly cajoling the players in one form or another to avoid violations of the rules and his very presence and mannerisms can often prevent sloppy play.

Remarkably, the precise viewpoint and philosophy appear in Hill's fascinating book, *Give A Little Whistle; The Recollections Of A Remarkable Referee:*

> You see, I just don't buy this point that is so often made even today that the best referee is the referee who is not noticed. I can see what is being said by that, but what is usually being ignored is that it is his skill as a referee that has made him not noticed. He has quite probably talked to both teams before the game, run alongside players and talked to them during the game . . . to say you've not noticed him infers that the referee is only an arbitrator, if that's the word; that he is merely there to react to situations. No, I believe you are the orchestra leader on many occasions; you are the man who can create the mood of that game.

Under both college and high school rules, the most heinous offense is, of course, charging the goal keeper who is in possession of the ball. Such an intentional action calls for ejection without any cautions or warnings. The NCAA College rule reads as follows:

The referee shall eject without previous caution any player who, with obvious intent, violently fouled the goalkeeper who is in possession of the ball in his own penalty area.

The approved college ruling requires that ejection without caution be applied only in cases where charging the goalkeeper who is holding the ball is both intentional and violent. The High School Federation rule states:

"An official shall remove, without caution, any player who intentionally charges the goalkeeper in possession of the ball."

Evidently, high school rules require only an intentional charging of the goalkeeper in possession of the ball to mandate ejection of that player.

The NCAA rule book neatly lays out how our famous reasonable referee reacts to the offenses of deliberate fouls and dangerous play:

Deliberate tripping, kicking, striking, spitting or jumping at an opponent or attempting to do same is dangerous and *liable to cause injury,* which compels the referee to caution the offending player that a repetition will necessitate the player's being ordered off the field (emphasis supplied).

In view of these dictates of the rules, be careful to, in fact, penalize any and all deliberate attempts or completions of the acts of tripping, kicking, striking, spitting, etc. If you do not penalize and an injury occurs, the injured player's attorney doesn't have to look too much farther than your own code of conduct, i.e., the rule book, to show that a reasonable referee would have taken note of what things are liable to cause injury. That is to say, the direct free-kick you will award for these acts must be accompanied by the appropriate cautions to the offending players.

How about the player or coach who decides to let all those interested know that you, the official, are the cause of whatever is going wrong with his team that day? As all soccer people know, unsportsmanlike conduct infractions, as well as a host of other violations, are indicated in soccer by an official displaying one or both of two colored cards. A *yellow* card means a caution to a player indicating that offense has been committed, that there is a penalty and that a further offense will result in disqualification. A *red* card indicating that the offender is immediately barred from further participation in the game. (In Switzerland a green card is also used to summon a coach and trainer on the field to assist an injured player.) These colored cards supposedly were born of the language barrier which was present when teams of different nationalities would meet. Of course, many of the insults and attacks on our calls as officials are delivered by the perpetrator in somewhat of a universal language. But that fact, of course, is neither here nor there.

There are as many approaches to game control as there are

There are as many approaches to game control as there are soccer referees.

soccer referees. Sadly, the violence that has plagued soccer fields the world over has made its presence felt in America at all levels of competition.

You must, of course, make it clear by your words and actions that you will not tolerate unnecessary roughness or unsportsmanlike acts. There are days, of course, when all the top referees in the world couldn't prevent the teams from brawling instead of playing soccer. However, if you are alert and have the ability to move quickly, you can often "head off at the pass" any players who seem to be hell bent on rearranging the faces of their opponents. I wouldn't recommend, however, taking a leaf from the book of one soccer referee in England who, Gordon Hill reports,

... before a big match, would grab known offenders by the scruff of the neck and tell them: "Any nonsense from you today, and I'll bloody well have you off." He would really make a song and dance about it. (p. 136)

Thankfully the National Federation has gotten away from the practice of requiring officials to display the appropriate card by holding it over the offending player's head. The card requirement is simply that the card be held overhead and ostensibly means overhead of the official who is holding the card and indicate the player in such a fashion that he will be identified to the coach, the scorer and the other officials. The NCAA specified that the appropriate card be displayed. There is also the direction in college competition that an ejectee must leave the field and be far enough away so as not to be a disruptive influence on the game.

WEATHER OR NOT

All of our outdoor sports must cause their officials to look skyward on occasion. Soccer, of course, is no exception. There will be time when weather poses a danger to participants and you must use your good common sense as a guide in suspending play. Unfortunately, neither rules code we have discussed is of much help. The terminology in both codes speaks of only "the elements" giving the referee power to suspend play or terminate the game when the elements require. You will have read this before if you are a baseball umpire: if you are playing soccer outdoors, and you see lightning anywhere, suspend play immediately. If you are the referee, suspend play immediately and don't take any nonsense from anyone. Retreat without delay to your car or room. If you are a linesman, do not permit play to continue but report to the referee immediately that you have seen lightning and that play must be suspended. I cannot emphasize it enough; don't take any chances with lightning!

8

CHECK-UP FOR WRESTLING OFFICIALS

The legal check-ups have been presented to you in alphabetical order. In these pages, wrestling is, as the saying goes, last but not least.

Officiating wrestling is quite unlike the other sports we have discussed. And it follows that in many respects the legal exposure of wrestling officials is unique and set apart from the legal exposure facing officials in the other team sports. Wrestling is the team sport officiated, for the most part, by one man.

That wrestling presents a different set of problems for its officials in terms of legal exposure is so for several reasons. As mentioned above, the most obvious is that wrestling officials often work alone, that is to say, in a crew of one referee. Secondly, the wrestling referee supervises a playing area considerably smaller than any of the other sports we have discussed. The area of concentration on which he focuses is extremely narrow. At the same time, the playing action in wrestling involves almost continuous bodily contact between the opponents who, by the very nature of the sport, are matching their strength, agility and endurance head to head against each other, rather than manipulating some foreign object such as a ball, a bat or a goal type apparatus.

Thus, relatively speaking, there is considerable potential for physical injuries to occur for which an official may be held liable. Indeed, Pennsylvania State University's National Athletic Injury Illness Reporting System's statistics on college sports during the 1977-78 season indicate that, of all the intercollegiate sports, wrestling presented the highest risk of injury in that 29.6% of college wrestlers sustained a significant injury or illness during the season. Why, then, is the injury factor so very significant, in terms of legal liability, for wrestling officials? A comparison with some of our other sports gives us the answer. There is little that a football official can do to prevent a spear or unnecessary rough and malicious tackle the first time it happens. The official can, of course, penalize, and, in so doing will cement his actions as a reasonable official, so if a player is later injured, his claim that the official was negligent will be refuted by evidence that the official did penalize appropriately for the infraction. Similarly, a baseball umpire can eject a pitcher for throwing at a batter's head or not, and this posture will be a significant factor in whether he is culpable in a court of law should an injury later occur.

But, in wrestling, the opponents are at each other right from the start! If an illegal hold is not detected by the official early enough, it is too late to penalize a wrestler after his opponent's spinal column has snapped. The official must view the action and intercede, using all the judgment he can bring to bear on the situation, when a hold goes over the line into the illegal and dangerous area.

Another unique aspect of officiating wrestling is the fact that the referee begins officiating in earnest long before his whistle sounds to start the match. While it is true that officials in most sports have a number of important tasks to perform before the event actually commences, in no sport that we have discussed are these duties more complex or demanding than in wrestling.

First of all, in many states the referee is responsible to weigh-in the wrestlers. This, of course, means that the referee will have to arrive in time to review the weigh-in schedule, check the scales, and conduct the weigh-in so the weight classes are established for each competitor.

Therefore, if you are in a state or league which requires you as referee to conduct the weigh-in, make sure that you do it properly in accordance with the rules. If you have failed to do any of the things necessary for the conduct of a proper weigh-in and later on during the match a wrestler is injured, a claim may be made against you that the wrestler wrestled out of his weight class due to some error in the weigh-in procedure, was injured, and that injury was in some degree caused by a wrestler competing against an opponent against whom he should not have been competing.

Remember that in college competition a wrestler may wrestle in any weight class above the one for which he weighed in.

Under high school rules, a wrestler may wrestle 1 but not more than 1 weight class above that class for which his actual stripped weight at the time of weigh-in qualifies him. Also, you should know the prescribed growth allowance, which is two pounds to each weight class beginning December 25 until February 1. Starting February 1, an additional pound is added. On March 1, an additional pound is added for the remainder of the season.

College rules provide for a growth allowance of 3 lbs. in November and December, 2 lbs. in January, and 1 lb in February, with the exception of qualifying tournaments which are scratch weight.

In high school competition, be careful to watch for not only the ringer who wrestles at 148, carrying a weight of 172, but also the swing-man, who the coach dispatches to wrestle unlimited but who really weighs 137. This could happen for a variety of reasons, all of them bad. If it does, and an injury occurs due to one wrestler being severely overmanned, you may well find yourself #1 on the list of defendants in a lawsuit. High school rules now specificially provide that any wrestler shifting to a higher weight class must have his *exact*

The National Federation Weight Classifications are as follows:

98 lbs.
105 lbs.
112 lbs.
119 lbs.
126 lbs.
132 lbs.
138 lbs.
145 lbs.
155 lbs.
167 lbs.
185 lbs.
Unlimited (min. 185 lbs.)

The NCAA weight classifications differ somewhat from those used in high school:

118 lbs.
126 lbs.
134 lbs.
142 lbs.
150 bs.
158 lbs.
167 lbs.
177 lbs.
190 lbs.
Unlimited (min. 177 lbs.)

weight certified at the time of weigh-in. This provision gives you some ammunition with which to play off potential legal liability. But you must do your job before the competition begins. What this means is the time to inquire as to any juggling is at weigh-in. In this way, if anyone is going to be shifted more than one weight class upwards, you can nail down the exact weight and thereby avoid a problem later on.

In NCAA wrestling, due to the travel time involved, weigh-ins are typically accomplished early in the day and certified to by affidavit of athletic directors. In this instance, you have no control over the situation.

The wrestling official should be sensitive to the fact that a wrestler must have at least one hour's rest between matches if he is to wrestle two matches during the day.

Once weigh-in has been accomplished, the referee is then required to visit both locker rooms for the purpose of checking the contestants for proper uniforms, grooming, and any physiological problems such as communicable diseases, skin conditions, foreign substances or objectionable pads. High School Federation rules require that wrestlers be clean shaven, with sideburns no lower than earlobe level, and hair trimmed and well groomed. In college competition, neatly trimmed mustaches are permitted providing they don't extend below the line of the lower lip. Hair may not extend below the top of the collar, nor shall hair extend below the earlobe level. Fingernails must be short and smooth. No jewelry of any kind may be worn. Any taping which limits the full movement of a joint is prohibited; as is any equipment which is hard or abrasive, unless covered and padded. Shoes must be light, without heels and of a type suitable for wrestling. They shall reach above the ankle and must be laced through eyelets and not hooks. If anyone is chewing gum, tell them to take it out before wrestling.

As officials, we must remember also that High School Federation wrestling rules cite the presence of a communicable disease or other health problem as grounds for disqualification of a contestant. However, there is apparently no requirement under these rules that a physician be present, although it is recommended. If, upon visiting the locker room, it is apparent to you that one of the wrestlers is ill with a communicable disease, you would be wise to request a medical opinion. If a physician is present at the match site, there is absolutely no excuse for failing to involve the physician in this decision-making process.

Under no circumstances should you take upon yourself the responsibility of allowing the wrestler to participate if there is evidence at hand that he is afflicted with an infection which may be transmitted to his opponent or to others. While on the subject of disqualification, when working in tournament play, make sure that the conclusion time of each match is recorded in the official score book. Be sensitive to the fact that a wrestler must have at least one hour's rest between matches if he is to wrestle in two matches during the day. If this rule is violated, it's *your* fault.

If you are in tournament play, and you are not able to get to the locker room prior to the squads appearing on the floor, don't let that fact prevent you from accomplishing everything you have to. Remember, there can be half a dozen coaches on each side, qualified physicians from all schools, and everyone from athletic directors to principals at the site ready to cheer their teams on, but *you* are the one who will be the first to be blamed in court for not doing your job before and during the match or tournament.

So, if you're doing your job properly, by the time you have left the locker rooms, you will have noted each and every wrestler's grooming, uniform and equipment, even to the extent that each wrestler is attired in accordance with the rules, right down to his athletic supporter.

Once you're on the mat and your pregame inspection of wrestlers has been completed, you are ready to inspect the mat and surroundings to make certain that the playing area is such that the competition can be conducted safely. Let's take a look first at the mat itself. The mat and safety mat area must be of uniform thickness, not more than 4 inches thick and, according to the rules, must be thick enough to provide the shock absorbing qualities of a two inch thick hair felt mat. The wrestling area, if circular, must be at least 28 feet in diameter; if square, it must be at least 24 feet square. There must be attached to the wrestling area of the mat a safety mat area at least 5 feet wide. And, of course, the mat must be free of debris or foreign matter. In the higher levels of competition, you will almost never encounter a difficulty with mat specifications or size. However, in some junior league wrestling programs and various recreation departments sponsored competition, you may find makeshift mats employed for use. Be absolutely certain that they conform to the specifications of the rules.

If you run into such a mat that does not so conform, there is little you can do to defend your actions if you allow the match to occur and an injury results.

Also, be sure that there is at least 10 feet of space surrounding the mat without any obstruction. Also, there must be at least 10 feet between the mat and the officials' table. Pay attention to these requirements, for you are the sole representative of the governing body charged with enforcing the rules. If the benches are too close to the mat and insurrection breaks out among the troops, keep in mind that you as referee may well be asked to fund the medical war chest from your own pocket.

If you had entered the visiting team's dressing quarters first, and then proceeded to the home team, you will have given the visitors a chance to go out on the mat and begin their warm-ups. If you are lucky, in that fashion you can often avoid having both teams on the mat at the same time for warm-ups. Again, it will not always be possible to accomplish this, especially in tournaments, but it's worth trying for. If the teams take the mat separately, there is less chance of jockeying back and forth and abusive remarks which may lead to an unsportsmanlike confrontation before you even begin.

Once we're on the mat and wrestling has begun, complete and total concentration is the order of the day if you're the referee. While the match is going on, there is precious little in the way of "off time," for you to gather your thoughts, take a breather, or regroup yourself for the next play or maneuver. For, as we said, in wrestling there is no ball to go out of bounds; no huddles between downs, and, most critical, often there is no other official with whom to consult in the event of a difficult call or rule interpretation. You're charged with controlling opponents who seek to impose their strength on each other!

High School Federation Wrestling Rules clearly spell out that it is the *referee's* responsibility to caution a contestant who employs a potentially dangerous or illegal hold. And, the rule states that the referee must do this ". . . in order to prevent possible injury." This provision of the rule, Rule 3:1-11 concludes that:

> The referee shall stop such holds if possible before they reach the dangerous state. The offender must be penalized for an illegal hold.

Let's analyze this for a moment. As we said before, the football official can penalize a spear, or butt-block, by throwing a marker and calling a foul, all of which will, hopefully, deter the next player from attempting a similar tactic. The baseball umpire can eject the pitcher who throws a beanball in the hope that the reliever will not be so brazen. Basketball referees can call a tight game, in the expectation that players who are called for several fouls early in the game will be afraid of fouling out and therefore will elect to curb their rough early play in favor of remaining in the game.

But, in wrestling, the corresponding actions of the referee extend beyond the calling of a violation of the rules after the fact to the affirmative obligation to go one step further and intercede directly between opponents to prevent possible injury before it occurs. Needless to say, the impact of this type of responsibility imposed upon wrestling referees is a substantial factor in making wrestling officiating from a legal standpoint one of the sports with the greatest exposure for its officials.

In other words, if you do not act where appropriate to do whatever is necessary to do to prevent a dangerous maneuver from resulting in an injury, you may not have acted as a reasonable referee would, and therefore you may be liable!

Take, for example, the allegations made against the wrestling official in the recent case cited in "The Liability Trap," where we quoted from the report of the plaintiff's expert witness. There was, you will recall, outlined in some great detail all of the ways in which the referee could or should have prevented the injury to the plaintiff. This so-called expert listed at least nine things that he felt the referee either should have done and did not do or did and should not have done. In that case, the referee had to refute allegations that he was negligent in:

- encouraging the plaintiff wrestler to participate beyond his limits of endurance;
- failing to instruct the wrestlers in the rules and safety measures of the sport;

- that he did not abide by the rules of wrestling in that he did not take preventive measures to immediately stop potentially dangerous holds;
- allowing the plaintiff wrestler to start the match without having warmed up properly;
- allowing undue stress on the neck of the plaintiff wrestler;
- permitting the match to start without a physician being in attendance;
- permitting the plaintiff wrestler's opponent to exercise excessive force and engage in an illegal hold;
- that he breached a duty to see to it that the wrestlers were instructed;
- that he did not stop the match when it should have been apparent that the plaintiff wrestler was in distress and failed to instruct the wrestlers not to utilize illegal or excessively dangerous holds, nor go beyond the physical endurance of an opponent in apparent distress.

In one of the landmark court cases involving wrestling, discussed at some length in "The Liability Trap," you'll recall that the referee allowed his attention to be diverted for a moment when he noticed that two sections of the mat had become separated. He thereupon apparently attempted to reconnect the two sections, and, in so doing, took his eyes, for the briefest of periods, off the wrestlers. According to the testimony at trial, the plaintiff wrestler's opponent was attempting a roll to get in position for a pin and had applied, to that end, a half-nelson. Unfortunately, instead of trying to break the nelson by looking to his left and peeling, the plaintiff looked into the half-nelson and his head was caught. The point is, of course, whatever the wrestler did wrong and whatever tactical mistake he made, what could well have been a legal hold obviously became dangerous at some point. And, unfortunately, the referee did not intervene in time to prevent the tragic injury.

And yet, actions on the mat are not the exclusive source of potential liability for the wrestling official.

Equipment can be critical in preventing or lessening, or even aggravating, injuries.

Be wary of the displaced headgear covering a wrestler's eyes or interfering with breathing. If you attempt to manipulate the headgear back into position without stopping the match, you may not be successful and may place one of the wrestlers at a disadvantage, at best. At worst, you may aggravate the situation due to a quick movement of the wrestlers and cause the headgear to do more damage. For this reason, it's probably the better practice to wait until a particular maneuver has been completed and you're able to stop the match momentarily without placing either wrestler at a disadvantage. Also, if the wrestlers are near the edge of the mat, you had better be ready to prevent the inevitable thud caused by a wrestler striking the floor, stands, or officials' table if the wrestlers go out of bounds.

Even a relatively rare instance where a coach believes that you as referee have misapplied a rule can lead to untoward complications. The procedure is not unlike that used in football whereby the coach may request a time-out to review the rule application with the referee. The rules specify that the conference shall occur directly in front of the officials' table, and that both wrestlers are to remain on the 10 foot circle during this conference. If you are not using mat judges and therefore are the sole official working the match, be sure to direct both wrestlers to stay in the circle, and conduct your conference facing the mat, keeping both opponents at least in your peripheral vision. It is important that you don't turn your back on opponents who may engage in their own discussion as to the match in progress. This, of course, is a tall order, especially if you are working alone. But, like your old third grade teacher who seemed to have eyes in the back of her head with which she could deftly detect any violation of class discipline, all good officials maintain this trait to a large degree.

On the subject of mat judges, the debate over their use will probably never be resolved to everyone's satisfaction, and certainly the officials are the last ones to have any input into the decision of a particular conference or association on whether or not to employ one or more judges to assist the referee. For our purposes, if you're the referee, and you're given mat judges, use them!

National Federation Rules state that either mat judges or an assistant referee is permissable. In the case of mat judges, the Federation rules provide that mat judges remain on the outside of the mat, but are authorized to enter the mat area to stop a potentially dangerous situation. Also, the position of the mat judges is low to the ground, either kneeling or sitting. In this fashion, a mat judge who detects an infraction or otherwise disagrees with the referee, will stand. The referee may or may not honor this request. When both mat judges stand, the referee is obligated to stop the match as soon as practicable to confer with his assistants. Further, mat judges are authorized to direct the referee to award points for locked hands or grasping of clothing. And, finally, if both mat judges disagree with the referee, his decision will be reversed.

For those high schools using the assistant referee, the procedure is somewhat different. The assistant referee, unlike the mat judge, has the run of the house. He does not stay seated in one place, but rather complements the referee, deferring to the referee in the event of any disagreement. The NCAA rules simply recommend that one mat judge be assigned to assist the referee in tournament competition. The mat judge in college is comparable to the assistant referee in high school.

UNNECESSARY ROUGHNESS

This is easily recognizable and absolutely must be nipped in the bud, lest such roughness lead to complications. The National Federation High School Wrestling Manual and Case Book identifies 5 prime examples of unnecessary roughness:

- Biting, butting, kicking, hair pulling, elbowing, slapping or punching; forceful rips;
- any hold which is used for punishment alone;
- unnecessary force in applying "crossface";
- any intentional act which endangers life or limb.

In addition to this, you must know the illegal holds which, while not constituting unnecessary roughness, must similarly be disallowed by the competent wrestling official.The illegal holds are as follows:

- The manipulation by twisting or by force of the head or any limb beyond its normal limits of movement;
- Hammerlock above the right angle, or twisting hammerlock;
- Straight head-scissors;
- Full nelson from the front, rear or side;
- The overhead double arm bar;
- Headlock without an arm or leg encircled (except in the guillotine);
- Twisting kneelocks;
- Locking the hands behind the back in a double arm bar from the front, unless the hands are locked under the opponent's armpit;
- Grasping less than four fingers;
- Keylock;
- Double wristlock with pressure applied parallel to the long axis of the body;
- Salto or suplay or any variation which meets slam criteria; (NCAA: Full back suplay and overscissors)
- Body slam;
- Neck wrench;
- Intentional drill or forceful fall-back;
- Strangle holds;
- Any hold with pressure over mouth,nose or throat which restricts breathing or circulation.

Remember that, in wrestling, *an injury, no matter how sustained, causes the match to be stopped immediately.* There is no room for compromise or interpretation on this one. The rule is clear and unequivocal. You as referee had better be firm in enforcing this rule also, if you want to stay on the mat and out of court. Like other sports, there is no completion of a play to wait for, no lag period when all further action has stopped. There is only the requirement that the official, or any one of them, recognize that one of the participants is injured and stop the match immediately. Don't make a mistake on this. Few things or maxims in the sports discussed in these pages are as simple or as important.

Of course, *how* the wrestler is injured will govern what you do immediately following the stoppage of play. Federation wrestling rules distinguish between a contestant being injured as the result of an illegal action of opponent and a legal action of opponent.

If the wrestler is injured due to a legal hold, the time taken for the wrestler to regroup and for a determination to be made if he can recover is known as injury time. There is a maximum of two minutes allowed for this purpose and the time is cumulative. That is to say, if wrestler requires the full two minutes before resuming the match, if he is injured again by a legal hold, he must default as he would have no injury time left in that instance.

The situation is much different when you have stopped the match because a wrestler was injured by his opponent employing an illegal hold. In that case, the offended injured party is permitted two minutes recovery time. However, if the wrestler is unable to continue wrestling after his two minute recovery time has expired, the match would be defaulted in his favor.

In either case, the time period with which you are working, at least the first time you stop the match, is two minutes. In addition, National Federation wrestling rules prohibit back to back recovery and injury time-outs.

If a wrestler intentionally attempts to injure his opponent, he must be disqualified. And, like baseball, if a wrestler is rendered unconscious, the physician in attendance at the match must authorize that wrestler's return to action.

On the subject of doctors, remember that the physician in attendance has the last word on withholding a wrestler from competition, whether or not loss of consciousness occurs.

NCAA college rules are a little more specific regarding the role of a physician. If you're a college referee, be familiar with Rule 7-5:6, which outlines that a wrestler who is rendered unconscious needs the approval of a physician to resume wrestling, just as in high school. The rule then goes on to state:

Similarly, a contestant who received a serious injury to the head, neck or spinal column must have a physician's approval before he may continue to compete.

Also, you should know that *nose bleeds* are treated differently in high school and college. In High School Federation competition, nose bleeds are not considered injuries in the sense that injury time-out is charged against a wrestler. In NCAA play, neither nose bleeds or any other excessive bleeding is treated as an injury time-out without the recording of time. In either case, there is no set limit on the number or duration of times-out in the event of nose bleeds. Therefore, as referee, you have discretion. If you are going to make a mistake here, be sure to err on the side of *granting* the time-out and allowing a wrestler with a nose bleed sufficient time to ameliorate his condition.

NCAA college rules require you to remain near an injured wrestler for the purpose of penalizing in the event that the coach engages in communication which can be regarded as coaching. If you are working a college match, remember that, just as in high school wrestling, a coach is permitted to attend to the needs of his injured wrestler. Although you cannot permit coaching during the injury time-out, don't look for trouble on this one. Any attempt by you to limit the coach in conversing with his wrestler in an effort to determine whether or not the wrestler should continue may be misconstrued later on should the wrestler become severely injured and bring a lawsuit against you. And, remember that there are no similar restrictions on the opposing coach during an injury time-out.

As you know by now, the point is to minimize the chance of legal exposure. Be reasonable and compassionate in dealing with injuries. It's not for you to determine if a wrestler is faking the injury.

9

AFTER THE GAME

During the game, be firm, be fair, and be decisive. After the game, be gone. Be gone and be quiet. More about "be quiet" later. But first, let's deal with "be gone."

It sounds simple, doesn't it? Yet, surprisingly, many officials make a practice of chasing basketballs, holding extended conversations with scorekeepers or others, or attempting to bid a cordial farewell to one coach or the other. The point is, you and your partner or partners should be looking for each other at games' end and, having made eye contact, leave the field or court together. Many younger officials make the grave mistake of strolling over to a coach after a game to exchange pleasantries, perhaps in the hope of receiving a compliment, perhaps in the hope of currying some kind of favor which will lead to future assignments, or perhaps out of a friendly and affable nature. Whatever the reason, if you find yourself walking over to "throw the bull" after the game with either coach, you're doing the wrong thing for any number of reasons.

If there has been some controversy surrounding the game and you anticipate a difficult situation, be wary of anyone who attempts to detain you by posing questions about a play or incident. If that person is a coach or administrator with whom you might have occasion to speak at other times during the game, do not be lulled into standing around and letting an argument occur. If you are able to answer a polite question from a coach while continuing your walk to your dressing room, do so. Remember that nothing will be gained by trying to convince a losing coach that your call was right and he has nothing to complain about. If the coach is abusive or begins to gesticulate in a manner that may give spectators the impression that he isn't too pleased with you, make no remarks whatever and proceed, with your partners, to your dressing room. The key here is to keep moving. Remember, when the game is over, your job is over.

To repeat, when the game is over, the experienced official, almost by reflex, takes the following steps immediately and without delay: removes lanyard, if any, from neck and places it in pocket; locates all members of his crew and keeps his eyes open, focused on the other members until all come together for the purpose of leaving the field or arena. Then, all will leave the enclosure together and proceed directly to the locker room.

Do not depend on security personnel or police officers assigned to the game. This is not to say that in many situations uniformed security personnel and police have not pulled many an official out of what could have been an ugly scene, but simply a reminder not to depend on anyone other than your brother officials.

The official's manuals for some of our sports deal briefly with this topic. The Collegiate Commissioners Association Basketball Officiating Manual requires officials to leave the court together at the end of the game and goes on to state this regulation:

SECTION 65.
Officials should neither seek nor avoid coaches, nor permit them to enter their dressing room. They should refrain from any discussion regarding their judgments during the game and should issue no statements to the media except for clarification of rules.

The National Federation Football Official's Manual similarly directs that all officials leave the field together and goes on to state:
Neither avoid nor seek to contact coaches. Do not discuss the game on the field and do not make any public statement about the game to the news media. If there has been any flagrant irregularity, report it as soon as possible to the State Association Office.

In similar fashion, the National Federation Baseball Umpire's Manual instructs high school umpires to leave the field together and cautions that "it is not advisable to discuss the game with anyone."

Now, let's talk about "be quiet." As the old football coach used to say, whenever you throw a pass, three things can happen, two of them bad. Similarly, after the game, when you are on your way off the playing enclosure, if you are challenged, heckled, insulted or your person is violated and you respond in kind, several things can happen, all of them bad.

However tempting it may be to put an ignorant spectator in his place by a sharp retort, the only thing you are doing is attaching significance to your assailant's remarks by responding to him. More importantly, the practice of engaging in a give and take with a spectator may well blossom into a full scale confrontation resulting in the necessity for you to defend yourself physically. If this happens, you may be the one charged with assault! I can't emphasize the point enough; don't waste your breath and risk injury or a lawsuit by speaking when you are not obligated to do so.

HANDLING THE MEDIA

A newspaper executive once did an informal survey of how a new competitor was doing on the stands by placing an observer across the street from a busy newsstand at rush hour. He found a curious thing. Many people would purchase a newspaper only to tuck the sports section under their arms and discard the remainder of the paper. Athletes, professional and amateur, sell newspapers. Officials do *not*—and they're not supposed to.

If you're a novice official, you probably won't be getting too many phone calls from the press relative to controversial plays in a game you had worked. And by the time you get to the level where the newspapers may come knocking on your door to get your version, you'll probably know better. But, anyway, in case it happens to you, remember that you can be perfectly candid and accurate in giving your account of a disputed play to the press, only to have your words inaccurately quoted or paraphrased, with the result that it would appear to a knowledgeable person reading the article that you either (a) misapplied the rule; (b) exercised poor judgment or mechanics; or, worst of all, (c) entertained a bias against the team, player or coach, or both.

More importantly, you should realize that the deck is stacked against you in terms of the loser of the game or match looking to you as a reason why he lost. If you are going to respond to a reporter's questions in terms of defending your call or non-call in a game or your application of a rule, remember that the losing team will have full opportunity to explain *your* mistakes in great detail. The same opportunity will not be extended to you to explain the losing team's mistakes in similar detail.

All officials acknowledge that it would be very poor practice for an official to give the media an account of all the times when the losing coach should have gone for the field goal instead of the touchdown, or pinch-hit for the pitcher who gave up 17 runs to the bottom of the 5th.

The question again boils down to our specific function as officials, a function which is unique and stands apart from all other functions in athletic competition.

Additionally, officials, coaches, and players are subject to the same human frailties as everyone else. Personality conflicts often surface; and the integrity of the official depends to a great extent on the fact that personality conflicts with a particular player or coach ought not affect the outcome of a contest. Therefore, commentary to the media will only accentuate and highlight any personal animosity that exists between the official and the player or coach. The effect may be to create the impression that the official may be less than objective in a future contest. All of this can be most easily avoided by a quick and fair explanation that it is considered inappropriate for an official to make public statements concerning any game he has officiated. Members of the press may not agree, but no one walks in our shoes as officials. That's why I can't emphasize enough; speak only with those with whom you are obligated to speak as a condition of your engagement as an official. To achieve professionalism in officiating, like in any other area, requires a high degree of common sense. And, common sense tells us that we ought not to inject ourselves gratuitously, lest it diminish our effectiveness as officials.

An additional consideration is comparable to the area of physical assaults on officials. In Chapter 10, there is a discussion of the necessity for an official to remain in a passive role in the event he is physically assaulted, lest the impression be made that the assault was a fight and not a unilateral attack.

In the same way, if you engage in verbal jousting with a coach or player in print or on the airways, you could find yourself in a situation where you may be the defendant in a lawsuit charging you with libel or slander, or you may be in a position of having a potential claim for defamation only to have a counterclaim filed against you alleging the same thing! This can happen, and has!

Beyond these considerations is the effect your post-game statements may have in proving that you should be held legally liable for an injury to a participant. If there has been any injury in a game or match you had worked, remember that the injured party may retain an attorney for the purpose of bringing a lawsuit against you, alleging that your negligence was the cause of his injuries and asking you to respond in damages. If this happens, you may be contacted by an investigator who will seek to extract from you a statement, either orally or in writing, as to what happened during the game. If you make such a statement, remember what they used to say on "Dragnet"; anything you say may and will be used against you in court! Sometimes, you may be asked to give a statement to an insurance company who is responsible for making medical payments to an injured person. Remember that you are under no obligation to give any statements to any outsider concerning an injury. Instead, refer all such requests to your attorney, association or commissioner who assigned you the game.

In any case, don't do what one high school wrestling referee did on the day following a match in which one of the wrestlers became paralyzed as a result of his participation in the match. This official gave a written statement conceding that he took his eyes off the wrestlers momentarily. The official later explained that he was led to believe that his statement was necessary in order to qualify the injured wrestler for financial assistance from a crippled children's fund. Remember this: The motives may be perfectly leigitimate and above board, but your statement can later be used against you and therefore, before making any statement to anyone, you need legal advice.

When post-game or match observations are required, make them count. Direct any comments to the authority who assigned you the game or to your official's association through its reporting procedure. There is an art to even this phase of officiating, as we shall see.

The only valid reason any official has to make public observations about a game he has officiated, verbal or written, is to achieve an objective of correcting a situation where there is evidence of inept or improper administration of the event which presents a danger to game officials or others.

FIGURE 1.

SPECIAL REPORT FROM ATHLETIC OFFICIAL
TO
THE HIGH SCHOOL PRINCIPAL AND THE IHSA OFFICE

This form is to be used to report any matter concerning high school athletic contests that merit the attention of the high school principal. It shall be used to report phases of the athletic program which the school should **immediately** attempt to improve. It may also be used to report an exceptionally good job of game administration. All instances involving unsportsmanlike conduct on the part of coaches, players, or fans should be reported on this form. Prompt reporting of problems by officials will prevent further incidents.

This form is to be filled out in triplicate and signed by the official. The yellow copy is to be sent to the principal, the white copy to the IHSA Office, the blue copy to be retained by the official.

Report on .... concerning a Boys ....
                        (School)   Girls   (Sport)

contest between .... High School, ... Ill., and
                          (Home School)

.... High School, ... Ill., on ....
        (Visiting School)   (Date)

Specific matter being reported:

Explanation or Comment:

(Use other side if necessary)

Date .... Signed ....
                                                              (IHSA Boys Athletic Official)

Address ....

SEND TO IHSA OFFICE

If, then, you are placed in an untoward position after a game at the hands of either participants or spectators, the action you take to invoke league or conference disciplinary or corrective procedures will of course vary greatly. If you are working a high school game, you will most likely have occasion to deal, directly or indirectly, with your state high school interscholastic athletic association. In those states which register officials directly for approval to work high school contests, the procedure may be somewhat different than in states where high school officiating is a function of an organization under contract to the governing state high school athletic association. Procedures range from the informal to the very formal. Several states use specially designed forms to encourage officials to report instances of unsportsmanlike behavior or worse. See Figure 1.

The form entitled "Special Report from Athletic Official to the High School Principal and the IHSA Office" is a 3-part form wherein the official is instructed to send one copy to the principal of the school involved and another copy to the Illinois High School Association Office, while retaining one copy for himself.

The state high school activities association in Missouri goes so far as to publish a manual outlining the responsibilities of officials and the high schools, This manual is reproduced in its entirety in Appendix A. It's well worth your reading. Whatever the particular method for reporting is, remember this: The basic premise is that you report a bad incident according to the procedure in the league or conference you are working and to no one else. Again, it's an extension of our basic premise that you are an official and only an official. As such, you speak and communicate only according to the dictates of your profession. This will avoid needless difficulties, such as needless exposure to lawsuits for slander and later assertions by persons who should know better, that you may entertain a bias against a particular team, player, coach or administration. These items will of course negatively reflect upon your professional standing. Why have it happen when you can so easily avoid it?

All in all, the regulations governing the types of things officials are advised to formally report differ widely for both high school and college officials. In some states, high school officials have been required to report the calling of all technical fouls for unsportsmanlike conduct. In other states, any ejection of a player or coach is sufficient to require an official to make a report of the incident. Other states are mysteriously vague and do not issue any guidelines more specific than the general statement found in the National Federation Officiating Manuals to report any flagrant irregularity in connection with the contest.

Some college conferences require their football referees to submit a detailed report after every game. In this report would of course be included any unsportsmanlike incidents that occurred.

The California Interscholastic Federation, Southern Section, requires officials to report crowd control or unsportsmanlike conduct problems, as well as ejections of coaches, to the area assignment coordinator of officials within 24 hours after the game. Beyond that, ejections of coaches must be reported and followed up with a written report.

At that point, the coach is banned from coaching until the principal of his school files a letter of explanation indicating the action he has taken to prevent a recurrence of the situation.

Other states deal with reports of unsportsmanlike conduct on an ad hoc basis.

In addition to the statistical information to be garnered from these reports, problem coaches can be identified and dealt with. Remember that each time an official takes the initiative to report a coach or player or an administrator who has abused an official, a permanent record is created. This is important. Many a disciplinary hearing has been concluded by a committee chairman or commissioner or hearing examiner declining to penalize a player, coach or institution due to the fact that they had had no prior reports and considered the violation a first offense, where in fact the incident may have been the coach's 18th offense, but the first one that anyone in a position of authority knew about. This is our fault as officials.

This is not to say that you should be eager to report any coach who looks cross-eyed at you. On the other hand, remember that the coach who barges into your locker room after the game and challenges you to settle your differences in the parking lot may, if you do

FIGURE 2.

Dear Leon:

This was a JV football match between Springfield and Decatur on September 20. The incident involved a fan who came onto the field and bumped me intentionally and then punched me in the mouth and shoulder.

There were late hits in the game and I warned three Decatur players that I would throw a flag if there were any more. Also, the coach from Decatur came on to the field during the second period and told me that the principal was in the stands and I wouldn't work at the school again unless I was able to control the game.

Then at the time out the Decatur coach came on the field again and told me and Willis Smith, my partner, to call it the same at both ends of the field. I feel that I have been a good official in that I have officiated varsity football for 9 years and I never had a player or fan punch me before. I have worked in the class II playoffs 2 years ago and was an alternate in the Valley Conference for their playoff games. I officiate baseball also and have been an umpire for more than 6 years. This is the first time I have experienced such cursing on the field and don't think it is right for a parent to be allowed to do this, especially when the principal is there. I will be available to meet with the fan who had to let his fists do his talking for him instead of trying to reason things out with me.

nothing about it, carry his threats one step further with the next official to work his game.

When it is necessary to render a report, unless you have experience as a commissioner or supervisor,or have been in a position to review past reports that have been completed by major college officials, you should consult your association's attorney or secretary prior to submitting your report of unsportsmanlike conduct. There is a right way and a wrong way to prepare these reports.

One of the major mistakes made by officials in preparing such a report is that they often seek to decry the unsportsmanlike acts by submitting a resume of their own officiating prowess and achievements, as if somehow to say: "It wasn't my fault. I am a good official. I've worked here, there and the other place and everybody likes me."

This is, of course, antithetical to the very purpose of such reports. The idea of an official reporting a coach, administrator, player or school is to put the onus on the unsportsmanlike party and to make the appropriate administrative machinery aware of the situation. Far too many officials, having been victimized by player or coach or spectator violence, place *themselves* on trial needlessly.

FIGURE 3.

REPORT OF GAME OFFICIALS:
Date: September 20, 1975
Game: Springfield-Decatur JV
Officials Involved: Willie Smith, Joe Stanhope and Frank Jones.

Mr. Carlton Price, Secretary
Ball Officials Association
Baltimore

Dear Carl:
Frank Jones, Willis Smith and I officiated the JV football game on September 20, 1975 between Decatur High School and Springfield High School played at Decatur's home field.
In the first quarter, Decatur player #67, one Linus, was penalized for unnecessary roughness by reason of the fact that he tackled his opponent out of bounds. Two plays later, #67 was again penalized for spearing and ejected from the game by me. At half time, an individual descended from the bleachers, whereupon he approached me and my officiating partners, who were leaving the field together to await the half time intermission. At that point, the individual from the stands identified himself as #67's father and said: "You son of a bitch, don't you ever throw a flag on my son again." At that point, we had passed him and I felt a blow to the back of my neck, followed by a punch which hit me just over the left eye, knocking me to the ground. Personnel from Decatur and from the other school quickly came over and took the individual away from us. Thereafter, I have notified the police and signed a criminal complaint against this individual after the police arrived at the scene.

Figure 2 is an example of a report that is improperly prepared. Note the following:

- The official indicates all the things he did wrong and failed to do during the game.
- The official admits to his supervisor that he did not properly apply the rules governing unsportsmanlike conduct;
- The official gives his officiating history which has nothing at all to do with the situation he is reporting;
- The official spouts platitudes, all extraneous and detracting from the issue at hand.

Figure 3 is an example of a properly completed official's report. Note that:

- The unsportsmanlike acts complained of are set forth unemotionally and without any exaggeration or commentary;
- The official does not take a defensive position;
- The official does not recite a list of plaudits he had received trom others indicating what a great official he is;
- The official indicates that he has followed the proper officiating mechanics;
- The official indicates that he has enforced the letter and the spirit of the rules;
- The official sticks to the facts.

I've heard many officials say that it does no good to report an incident to the State High School Association because nothing ever happens. It ain't necessarily so. Ask Frank Spruiell, Commissioner of the Louisiana High School Athletic Association. At the National Federation annual meeting in 1974, Mr. Spruiell reported that his efforts to protect game officials resulted in a $90,000 lawsuit being filed against him and the Louisiana High School Athletic Association by a woman who was a spectator at a high school basketball game.

Evidently, her team lost. The officials' report indicated that immediately after the game the woman descended from the bleachers onto the basketball court and proceeded to chastise one of the officials, and while in the process grabbed his arm and physically detained him on the floor as an angry crowd milled about. The Sportsmanship Committee of the Louisiana High School Athletic Association held hearings which resulted in the woman spectator's school being placed on probation for one year, in addition to assessing a money fine and being informed that the school was forbidden to participate in any interscholastic athletic contests for one year with the woman in attendance.

All in all, it's unlikely that this woman will ever again accost a referee. For, according to the Louisiana Court of Appeals, the woman plaintiff claimed that she had

. . . been humiliated by the fact that principals of participating schools searched the audience for her before allowing Fenton (the high school where the incident occurred) to begin play. She alleges further that, at the Top-20 Basketball Tournament in March of 1974, Commissioner Spruiell informed the principal of Fenton High School that should Mrs. Watkins come into the coliseum "the game would be stopped and Fenton would be allowed 2 minutes to get the fan out of the coliseum or the game would be forfeited." She asserts abridgement of her rights of free speech and assembly, invasion of her privacy and damage to her reputation. Specifically, she alleges that she has been embarrassed and humiliated in the eyes of her neighbors and her own children by the ruling which brands her as being unsportsmanlike.

In dismissing Watkins' suit, the court agreed that the exercise of regulations to protect game officials was valid, and upheld the Association's decision.

Another incident, this time involving a high school football player assaulting an official, was replayed in Federal Court in Texas in 1973.[1] On November 10, 1972, a 17 year old high school football player named John Stock allegedly assaulted a referee after a high school football game. According to the official report of the case at 364 F. Supp. 362, the Fort Worth Football Officials' Association recommended to the governing league that Mr. Stock be prohibited from further participation in competitive sports. After the appropriate hearings, the Executive Board of the Texas Catholic Interscholastic League terminated the player's eligibility and also barred his school from competing for district honors in football the following season. An appeal was taken to the Executive Board of the League from this decision and the result was a modification permitting the player to again participate in winter and spring activities after January 1, 1974, provided that the high school principal and school counselor affirmed that the player's sense of fair play had improved. Suit was brought in the United States District Court for the Northern District of Texas by the 17-year old football player, alleging that he was denied his constitutional rights to play football. In ruling against the player, the federal judge succinctly stated at the time that the United States Constitution does not guarantee the right to play football.

It's true that all instances of conduct in amateur sports which place officials in danger of life and limb are not dealt with so forthrightly by the respective governing bodies. But, unless the official initiates the process of reporting the actions of players, coaches, spectators, or what have you, there is no initial input from which the process can be invoked. In other words, we as officials must initiate the process to give the system a chance to work. True, it doesn't always work. I have not seen statistics, nor do I know of any compiled on a nationwide basis to indicate that the disciplinary procedures regarding abuse of game officials at the high school level and below, even works a significant percentage of the time. But the point is, if we don't initiate the process, there's no chance that we can adequately protect ourselves.

DEFAMATION

It happens at least once a year. An official comes charging into the law office, clutching a letter written by an angry coach or booster club big wig to a Commissioner, or a newspaper article outlining 101 ways that the official caused the home town Bengals to lose the County Championship.

"They can't do this to me, can they? All the guys at work told me I should get a lawyer and sue!"

Recovery of damages for injuries to one's reputation, called in the law "defamation," is a form of legal action that, for reasons which we will presently discuss, is much more talked about than carried out.

The law governing defamation, popularly known as "libel," (in written form) and "slander" (in spoken form), is an ever-changing melange of somewhat complex principles balancing the constitutionally guaranteed right to free speech and expression against an individual's right to not have his good name tarnished by false statements.

This is one area of the law where the chances of your recovering damages as a plaintiff depend not only on what was done to you but who you are in relation to the community at large.

The essence of defamation is a false statement which tends to denigrate one in the eyes of his fellow citizens. In order to be actionable, the defamatory material must be communicated to a comprehending third party or parties.

Generally, slanderous utterances (spoken as opposed to written) in his business or professional career will enable the injured party to recover damages without the necessity for proving an actual out-of-pocket loss. Also included in this category is slander which imputes the commission of a crime.

With respect to defamatory material in written form, libel, a lawsuit may be successfully maintained without the necessity for proving actual pecuniary loss.

Additionally, as we have seen in discussing the liability of officials for their actions, any legal cause of action may be subject to certain *defenses,* which will defeat or mitigate the cause of action. The primary and most obvious defense to a lawsuit for slander or libel is *truth.* That is to say, a true statement cannot enable one to recover for libel or slander, no matter how devastating to the individual the fact is.

In other words, for example, if the subject of a lawsuit for libel was a newspaper account of a football game stating that referee John Smith is incompetent and does not know the rules of the game because he penalized the home team 20 yards for holding instead of 15, the court would have to decide whether or not John Smith did actually penalize the home team 20 yards for holding when the Rule Book says this is a 15 yard penalty. If the damaging statement of fact is true, John Smith will fail in his lawsuit against the newspaper. Truth is a defense to a lawsuit for libel or slander.

Another equally important defense to a defamation lawsuit brought by a referee or umpire is that of *fair comment*. Sports, like politics, are frequently the subjects of great public interest. Indeed, for most of our non-official friends, a goodly part of the enjoyment of sports is derived not from making the hook shot, pounding the running track, or swimming the laps, but rather from listening to the commentators on television, reading accounts of games and matches in the newspaper, and digesting magazine treatments, box scores and innumerable statistics comparing the relative prowess of the competitors. In matters of public interest, it is not uncommon for the media to offer opinions as to the competence or lack thereof of the athlete, and, as we all know too well, the officials!

As any official knows, referees and umpires are often the perfect alibi for a player who has "choked" in the clutch. All of this, as they say, sells papers. In a lawsuit for libel or slander, the court will distinguish between statements of *opinion* and statements of *fact*. Statements of opinion will generally be immune from prosecution for libel or slander as these statements are considered "fair comment" and an exercise of free speech protected by our Constitution. The reasoning here is, of course, that there is a right to comment upon matters of public interest, such as sporting events. This right to comment embraces opinions and criticism made in good faith as commentary upon the events being discussed.

Coupled with the defense of fair comment is the necessity for the court to determine the status of a plaintiff complaining of libel or slander with respect to the activity which is the subject of the lawsuit. For, as we have said, in the area of defamation, if you are a plaintiff, the extent to which you have interjected yourself, by virtue of a profession, activity or participation, in a particular event or series of events which generate considerable public interest will be determined by the court in order to resolve the issue of what, if any, protection you are entitled to in terms of comment and criticism of your work.

Referees and umpires have generally been considered by the courts as public figures within the meaning of general guidelines set down by the United States Supreme Court.[2] What this means in practical terms is that referees and umpires who officiate games in which there is sufficient public interest to generate media attention, must endure criticism and comment, not necessarily educated, accurate or justified, upon their work.

10

IF YOU ARE INJURED

There are two ways that you can be injured while officiating. You can be injured accidently. You can be injured intentionally.

What you are going to be able to do about it depends somewhat upon this distinction. Therefore, let's talk about them separately.

INTENTIONAL INJURY

One of my old criminology professors used to say that statistics on crime are like a woman's bikini. He went on to explain, "What they reveal is interesting, but what they hide is vital!" How much more so with the crime of assault upon referees and umpires.

Jim Brosnan, the old Cincinnati Reds pitcher, once wrote a book called *The Long Season.* If he were writing it about what we as officials go through, we might call it *The Open Season.*

Yet what about the assaults that don't get reported in the media? And, what about the cases that do gain some notoriety but result in the official and/or the local authorities declining to prosecute and/or the local authorities declining to prosecute the offender?

Although it happens at least once a year, it always amazes me when an official is struck and he refuses to demand a criminal prosecution of his assailant. Aren't those officials inviting future attacks upon themselves and the rest of us?

First, let's look at how this process works. Confusion abounds as to the redress an official has when violence is perpetrated upon him. There's nothing particularly complicated about it, but many officials are confused as to ways in which the legal system can help. There are things you need to know to protect yourself and to help your lawyer to protect you.

Did you ever notice what happens when a police officer is assaulted? There are so many charges lodged that the legal system gets several bites of the apple in an attempt to bag the offender. There is a good reason for this. Police officers, highly visible to the public and at once the keepers of the peace and scapegoats of society, are, like officials, subject to affronts on their safety and dignity, ranging from verbal insults to brutal and deadly violence. Were they not to protect their own brethren by doing all in their power to discourage and deter attacks on themselves, they would be unable to do an effective job of protecting the rest of us. The point is, like referees and umpires, police officers perform a necessary function in society. That's why, when a police officer gets assaulted, the list of charges against the assailant usually reads (dependent on local practice and state and local law variations) like this: assault and battery, atrocious assault, aggravated assault, mayhem, resisting an officer, surety of the peace, resisting arrest, interfering with a police officer, inciting to riot, disorderly conduct, assault with intent to maim, etc., etc.

In the event of players, coaches or even spectators using you, the official, as a punching bag or target for all kinds of flying objects, you must take immediate affirmative and decisive action; not necessarily in an effort to punish the offender for the sake of punishment or retribution, but rather to deter others from getting the same idea.

Anyway, if you are assaulted, there is more than one way, as your grandfather used to say, to skin a cat. The action of a person striking another is known in criminal law as a *battery*. The *assault* part is an intentional offer to injure another person, creating in the victim for that person a reasonable fear that he is about to be injured. Although the exact definitions and laws vary from locality to locality, the point is that the matter of one person intentionally striking or doing violence to another person is a matter of concern not only to the victim but to the State. Hence, a crime.

Although oftentimes no representative of the State in the form of a police officer will be present at that sandlot softball game where you get belted in the nose for calling some 12 year old out on strikes. Still, assault and battery, even against a zebra, is a criminal offense.

Though you may have a hard time convincing governmental authorities, it may be your job to see to it that the appropriate procedures are followed to ensure that the perpetrator must face a court of law to answer for his actions.

As important as criminal prosecution of an offender is in matters of assaults upon officials, such prosecutions are completely separate and apart from what lawyers call the tort aspect of an injurious act. What does this all mean? When you file a complaint or give information which results in a complaint being filed by police authorities against your attacker in the wake of an assault, the judge or jury hearing the matter will make a finding as to whether or not the individual is guilty of the crime or offense of assault and battery.

This may result in a fine, and, in extreme cases, probation or (rarely) a jail sentence. Also, the guilty party will have the dubious distinction of living with whatever criminal record is made of his conviction.

These matters, however, usually do not in and of themselves, result in compensating the injured party for medical bills, broken glasses, etc., and the loss of income, pain, suffering and humiliation.

This is where the civil remedy of a lawsuit comes into play.

In a civil lawsuit, it is the person aggrieved, the person injured through the intentional or negligent act of another who has a right to go into court and demand redress in the form of money. For this type of action, you'd best have an attorney. Not only will he be able to assist you in pressing your claim for damages, if appropriate, but he will be of invaluable assistance in coordinating the criminal prosecution of your assailant. We'll go into this presently.

So, you see, there are actually two prongs to your counter-attack if someone has the mistaken notion that because you put on a striped shirt you have become fair game.

The first prong is your right to file or have filed a criminal complaint, and the second prong is your right to bring a lawsuit in civil court against the offender. Let's see how these processes of the legal system work.

CRIMINAL CHARGES

It doesn't matter if you are working the Idaho State High School Boy's Basketball Semi-Finals or the Southern Florida Pee Wee Baseball League, if you are struck and a blow is landed, there are definite steps you must take, things you must do, and things you must not do. If a definite procedure is followed by the official facing such an unfortunate occurrence, the chances of justice prevailing are far greater.

First of all, we're going to assume that preceding the assault, you have done nothing that would cause anyone, such as a judge, to believe that the incident was a fight between an official and a player, coach, spectator, etc. If you have been holding a running conversation with your attacker, especially if that person is someone with whom you have no reason to be speaking as part of your official duties, such as a spectator, you have opened the door to unpleasant consequences. That's why, I cannot emphasize enough that you should speak only to those people to whom you must speak as part of your job as an official. Don't take on any extraneous roles. The best and safest way to deal with remarks from spectators is to pretend that you don't hear them. If you enter into a dialogue with these people, you have brought yourself to their level, you have made them and their nonsense a part of your life and you have acknowledged their presence as persons important enough to deserve your attention. None of these, of course, should be the case.

Let's take an example. You're working an underclass football game, played after school on a field where assorted spectators frequently wander to the sidelines. There is no security, no athletic director. The entire evidence of school administration present is embodied in the form of one 25 year old assistant football coach, who has enough trouble keeping track of his squad and what's going on in the field, so that he cannot be concerned with anything else.

A player, though junior high school age and seemingly not sufficiently equipped to make the judgment, indicates that, in his judgment, your mother and your father were never married. You throw a penalty marker and eject him from the game.

Whereupon, one of the spectators, obviously with a vested interest in the outcome of this battle of 14 year olds, comes charging out on the field, demanding to know why you kicked his son out of the game.

The moment of truth has arrived. Do not speak to this individual. You owe him no explanations, nor is it your job to explain your decisions to a misfit trespassing on your field and disrupting a school activity. Don't waste any energy on this individual. Don't make him a part of the game or your life. Don't acknowledge his presence, other than by taking the following immediate steps. In our example, we have postulated that there are no security or police on hand, nor is there an administrator from the school.

Therefore, you must go to the home coach, regardless of which team the spectator is following. Tell the coach to take whatever steps are necessary to get rid of the spectator immediately. Get with your partner or partners and wait until the home coach has accomplished this, making no remarks.

If the home team cannot clear the field for play or make suitable arrangements for security, the rules of each sport give you an appropriate remedy. But don't put yourself and your partners (and everyone else on hand) in needless jeopardy for the sake of a game.

Should the unthinkable happen anyway, and you or a partner are struck by a spectator, if, as in our example, there are no police on hand, telephone the police immediately. If there is any indication that there is actual physical injury to you, ask the police to send an ambulance with them.

This is not the time to be the spartan warrior, concerned that the game must go on and you're man enough so that a glancing blow can't phase you. On the contrary, a crime has been committed, and to ignore it, places every official working in greater danger.

If police are present at the game, ask the officer if he saw what happened and if his answer is yes, tell him you assume that he will take the appropriate action. Unfortunately, there is a trend in some areas to place a glass wall around a playing field or gymnasium and take the position that whatever happens on the field or court somehow is "part of the game," and therefore should not be interfered with by the legal system. Sadly, this attitude, in these violent times, spells murder for us as officials. Are we the last line of authority in a world where it is fashionable to challenge authority?

Most officials have the good sense and self control to keep their cool in the heat of battle, even if the battle involves blows being landed with the official on the receiving end. This is extremely important if you are to assert your legal rights and not be in a position to be criticized. In other words, what I am telling you is, use only such force as is necessary to protect yourself. Do not under any circumstances, fight back. If you do, the civil authorities might well conclude that what happened was a fight during a game. If you're into fighting, join the AAU. If you're an official, don't fight. Don't, in fact, do anything that would lead anyone to a conclusion that an attack upon you was a fight between you and a player, coach, fan, etc.

It almost goes without saying that, to reduce the chance of a physical assault on you, you must react in a calculated manner to any verbal assaults upon you. This means that you must remember who you are and where you are at all times. If you are an official, you are not paid to argue or speak with spectators. You are paid to speak with players, coaches, and administrators when necessary. It is not part of your job to explain calls, defend your actions, or otherwise interact with onlookers. A great many problems could be avoided if officials would remember to do the job, the whole job, and nothing but the job, excluding all else.

If there is a police officer at the field or in the gym, you will want to seek him out to inquire if he viewed the incident. If his answer is yes, tell him you expect that he will place the perpetrator under arrest and you will cooperate with him. If he exhibits any hesitancy to detain your attacker, make a written note of his shield number and name, if he's wearing a name plate, and tell him that you are immediately telephoning police headquarters since a crime has been committed, and if he isn't going to report it, you will. Do not, of course, argue with the police officer or attempt to interfere with any other activity he may be pursuing at the moment. It is well to remember that, although most police officers, particularly in the larger metropolitan areas, are trained to be courteous and responsive to the needs of the public, they, like officials, work under tremendous pressure. Therefore, while not attempting to complicate the officer's life, you must politely but firmly insist that he take proper action with respect to the assault. If he does not, make good your promise, telephone the police headquarters and report the crime immediately.

At this point, one of two things may happen: the police officer may request that you pile into a squad car to be driven to police head-quarters at the same time as your attacker for the purpose of giving statements and signing complaints. Tell the officer that, after you have received medical treatment, you will find your own way to head-quarters. The other procedure will simply be for the police to inform you that if you want to sign a complaint, you should come into head-quarters and they will take the information.

Do not, under any circumstances, agree to participate in any "dis-cussion" involving yourself, your attacker and the police. Sometimes, police will attempt to mediate what they consider a dispute that really doesn't rise to the level of criminal activity. The point is, of course, that a physical attack on a referee or umpire does rise to the level of crimi-nal activity, but if you, as victim, don't force the issue, all may be lost.

In either case, remember to immediately seek medical attention if there is any question in your mind that you may be injured. Thereaf-ter, you should telephone your attorney and the commissioner or office that assigned you the game. Next, you will want to sit down and write exactly what happened, giving as many details as possible (you were struck on the left side of the face with the attacker's right arm; the home coach was standing 2 feet away from you; the second baseman was directly behind you, etc., etc.). These details have a way of becoming hazy with the passage of even a little time, given the confusion often surrounding such an undisciplined activity as a physical assault. Therefore, it is vital that you capture as many of the details as you and your partner or partners can remember on paper. This will greatly aid the prosecuting attorney in his effort to convince the judge or jury of what actually happened.

Also, it is important that you write down the names of any and all persons who witnessed the event, either by name, if you know the name, or title or description, etc. The prosecuting attorney will need a list of these people to call as witnesses at time of trial, and will undoubtedly want to interview them beforehand.

As a rule, don't expect too much help from players, coaches, administrators or bystanders. It's fashionable and relatively safe to say "I didn't see." If you never quite believed that the stuff they told you in cadet classes about your partner being your only friend on the field or court, you will now.

Anyway, you will be met with varying degrees of enthusiasm by the police in assisting you in charging your attacker criminally for his crime.

Depending on local practice, several documents will have to be generated by the authorities, with your help. This is where your lawyer comes in. The arresting officer, or the desk officer, if police do not respond to the scene, will usually make out a preliminary report, known as an incident report, or log entry. From this document, a criminal complaint will be written, either by the police officer, a designated court clerk, or District Attorney. The complaint is simply a sworn statement alleging the violation of law committed with particulars included, and signed by someone having personal knowledge of the facts. It is preferable that the complaint be signed by a police officer, who is empowered to do so if he had actual knowledge of the assault.

In the case of a very serious assault upon you, where you are either seriously injured or a lethal weapon has been used, the procedure may be a little different. After arrest of the attacker, the prosecuting attorney may present the matter to a grand jury to seek an indictment, which will result in felony prosecution. A police officer who is present at your game and witnesses an assault upon you is empowered to make an arrest in most jurisdictions. There are, of course, other ways in which a criminal legal action can be commenced against the perpetrator of an assault. A warrant can be issued by a court directing that a person be arrested if there is evidence that a crime has been committed; or, upon the signing of a criminal complaint by a police officer or by any individual, a summons may be issued, directing a person charged with the crime to appear in court to have the charges read to him and provide for his defense.

In most cases, however, the procedure following an assault is as outlined, with a complaint being issued either by a police officer or by the victim, and the matter being tried in a local or municipal or police court.

It is at this stage, when the information is being taken by the authorities from which the documents are to be written that you need to be represented. If your official's Association or Board has an attorney, this is the time for him to swing into action. The reason for this is simple. If you give a statement to the police without having the advice of counsel or someone knowledgeable in how these matters are handled, the report of the incident, the resulting criminal complaint, and the ultimate disposition of the matter may be the opposite of what you intended, all because you did not follow proper precautions. In theory, when a crime or disorderly person's offense such as an assault and battery is committed, the victim of that crime or offense need not have his own counsel due to the fact that a crime is a crime against the people, against the State, and therefore the State will supply the legal mechanism to prosecute that crime in everyone's interest. That's why criminal legal actions are called: "State versus Smith," or "People versus Doe," rather than have the name of the victim in the title of the case.

In actual practice, however, as victims of many crimes and not just officials know, things can be quite different. This is true for a variety of reasons. What concerns us as officials is that, in the everyday scheme of things, people are so accustomed to the oft televised scene of coaches and managers ranting and raving at officials that they may regard assaults at the high school, college or sandlot level as simply "part of the game."

FIGURE 1

OFFENSE REPORT
Police Department
Township of Cherry Hill

PATROL USE			INVESTIGATING USE		RECORDS USE	
Adult Arr	[ ] 10	Det. Assig. _____		Arrest	[ ]
XCLR Adult	[ ] 20	Adult. Arr.	[ ] 10	CFS	[ ]
JUV Arr	[ ] 30	XCLR Adult	[ ] 20	Inc. Name	[ ]
XCLR Juv	[ ] 40	JUV. Arr.	[ ] 30	Known Offender	[ ]
Pending	[ ] 60	XCLR Juv	[ ] 40	Inc. Susp.	[ ]
Unfounded	[ ] 70	Pending	[ ] 60	Offense	[ ]
		Unfounded	[ ] 70	Property	[ ]
		Disp. Date _____		Vehicle	[ ]

01. Incident #	02. Offense Classification			03. Offense Code	04. U.C.R Code	05. Status	07. Grid
06. Location of Offense				08. Patrol Area	09. Shift	10. Date Reported	11. Badge # 12. Division

20. Person Reporting Incident: **Frank Smith** 21. Address: **21 Main St.,Anytown,Pa.** City State 22. Res. Phone: **722-3487** 23. Bus. Phone: **444-6655**

24. Victim Name (Last, First, Middle) Firm Name (if com.)		26. Res Phone		Offense Occurred	
☒ if same as #20				Earliest	Latest
25. Residence/ Bus Address	City State	27. Bus Phone		13. Date	15. Date

30. Victim's Age **31**	31 Sex **M**	32 Race **W**	33 Employer/School Address	28. Weather: **clear**	14. Time	16. Time

34. Witness #1 Name (Last, First, Middle)		29 Injured Yes [ ] No [ ]	Days of Week of Occurrence S M T W T F S
35. Witness #1 Address	City State	36. Res Phone	37. Bus Phone

38 Age	39 Sex	40 Employer/School	41 Address	City	State

42 Witness #2 Name		43. Address, City, State	44 Res Phone	45 Bus Phone

46. Witness #2 Description	Employer/School		Address	City	State
Age	Sex				

RECORD TYPE   I = Impounded   SK - Safe Keeping   D - Damaged   T - Towed   S - Stolen   R - Recovered   U = Used in Crime   L = Lost   F = Found   E = Evidence

47 Item Number	48. Record Type	49 Qty	50 Prop Type	51 Brand Make or Manufacturer	52 Model Name and Number	53 Description (Color Size)	54 Serial No or OAN	55 Value

56. Property Disposition		A Currency $	B Jewelry $	C Furs $	D Clothing $	E Misc $	18. Total Prop. Stolen $
	57 VCO	58 V YR	59 VMA	60 VMO	61 VST	62 LIC 63 LIY 64 LIS 65 LIT	

67. VIN	68 Other Identifying Marks	19. Stolen m/v Value $

69. NCIC #	70 SCIC #	71 Entered SCIC [ ] NCIC [ ]	72 Date	73 Time	74 ID #	75 Cancel NCIC [ ] SCIC [ ]	76 Date	77 Time	78 ID #
17. Stolen From (OR)	79 Owner Notified Yes [ ] No [ ]	80 ORI NOTIFIED Yes [ ] No [ ]	81 Name Person Notified			82 Date		83 Time	84 Name Making Notification

85 Suspect #1 Name **Joe Johnson**	Address **13 Market St.,Woodtown,Pa.**	City	State	Age **20**	Sex **M**	Race **W**	Ht **5'1"**	Wt	Hair **Br**	Eyes **Br**
86 Suspect #2 Name	Address	City	State	Age	Sex	Race	Ht	Wt	Hair	Eyes

87 Arrest Made Yes [ ] No [☒]	88 Victim ID OR Yes [ ] No [ ]	89 Additional Description Not Included In Block 103 to 114

90. Narrative

Mr. Frank Smith stated he was the umpire in the baseball league. Mr. Johnson disputed a close call and the argument ensued. Then a fight occurred between Mr. Johnson and the umpire.

91 Medical Examiner Notified	92 County Det. Notified	93 Pronounced Dead By	94 Time/Date	95 Location	96 Other Officers at Scene
97 Det Notified Yes [ ] No [ ]	98 Det on Scene Yes [ ] No [ ]	99 Crime Scene Unit Required Yes [ ] No [ ]	100 Other Reports Supplement [ ] UAR [ ] Removal [ ] Other [ ] Prop Receipt [ ] Statement [ ] Warrant [ ]		
101 Reporting Officer	Rank	Name	ID #	102 Reviewing Supervisor Rank Name ID #	

Signature	Signature	CHPD #112 REV 6/82

Consider, for example, what happened when one official, assaulted during a men's baseball league game by a player, voluntarily went in to police headquarters and gave information which resulted in the Incident Report depicted in Figure 1. Compare this with a correctly completed report depicted in Figure 2.

FIGURE 2

**OFFENSE REPORT
Police Department
Township of Cherry Hill**

PATROL USE		INVESTIGATING USE		RECORDS USE	
Adult Arr.	□ 10	Det. Assig.		Arrest	□
XCLR Adult	□ 20	Adult. Arr.	□ 10	CFS	□
JUV. Arr.	□ 30	XCLR Adult	□ 20	Inc. Name	□
XCLR Juv.	□ 40	JUV. Arr.	□ 30	Known Offender	□
Pending	□ 60	XCLR Juv.	□ 40	Inc. Susp.	□
Unfounded	□ 70	Pending	□ 60	Offense	□
		Unfounded	□ 70	Property	□
		Disp. Date		Vehicle	□

20. Person Reporting Incident: **Frank Smith** — 21 Address: **21 Main St.,Anytown,Oa.** — 22 Res Phone **722-3487** — 23 Bus Phone **444-6655**

34. Victim Name: **☒ if same as #20**

30. Victim's Age — 31. Sex **M** — 28 Weather **clear**

34. Witness #1 Name: **Mark Ryan**
35. Witness #1 Address: **100 Lindy Avenue,Springfield,Pa.**
38. Age **18** — 39. Sex **M** — 40. Employer/School **Milltown Board of Education** — 41 Address **Milltown Rd.,Milltown,Pa.**

85. Suspect #1 Name: **Joe Johnson** — Address **13 Market St.,Woodtown,Pa.** — Age **20** — Sex **M** — Race **W** — Ht **6'1"** — Hair **Br** — Eyes **Br**

90. Narrative: Complainant was officiating a baseball game at County Park when he stated he was attacked by a player after he had made a call, by means of the player punching him about the eye, neck, face and shoulders with his fists and poking him with the end of the bat.

CHPD #112   REV 6/82

When the case is called for trial, practice varies by jurisdiction. Normally, the State will supply a prosecuting attorney to represent the State prosecuting the allegations that an assault and battery was committed against you. This attorney usually has a title, either Prosecutor, or District Attorney. It is before the trial and sometimes during the trial that your own attorney can play a great part in seeing that justice is indeed done. For, although the theory is that the State is interested in prosecuting crime, oftentime prosecutors on a municipal court level, where most of these offenses will be tried, do not have any opportunity to review the cases they are to be presenting to the court beforehand and therefore, being unaware and unprepared, may give what appears to be a ball-field dispute less attention. This, as officials, we cannot afford. Your own attorney, by communicating with the office of the Prosecuting Attorney before trial, can apprise him of the facts and the significance of the matter to the community. In fact, in some jurisdictions, according to the preferences of the particular trial judge, where a private individual executes a complaint in the criminal court, that individual may have his private attorney prosecute the action in behalf of the State.

In any event, if you are injured due to an intentional act, have the fortitude to stand up for your rights. Don't walk away. Not only will you create the impression that you had it coming, but you will be doing a disservice to your brother officials.

ACCIDENTAL INJURIES

Officiating can be dangerous to your health! A wet spot on the basketball court; a divot behind home plate; a blitzing linebacker; an errant throw from the third baseman; or even a fist that misses its target are but a few of the ways in which you can be unintentionally injured while officiating. As we have seen in "The Liability Trap," an injury, no matter how serious or disabling, does not always mean that the injured party will recover damages in the courts should he choose to file a lawsuit. The fact that there is no question of an official's voluntary participation in the activity militates against the chances of an official recovering for accidental injuries occurring in the course of officiating.

Clearly, the ability of an official to recover damages for injuries sustained while officiating is severely limited by the legal doctrine of assumption of the risk, about which we spoke earlier. By the way, the legal case which is most often cited in support of this doctrine is that of *Murphy v. Steeplechase Amusement Company, Inc.*[1] The decision of the case was rendered by the eminent Judge Benjamin Cardozo. That case involved a plaintiff injured as a result of going on a ride, in an amusement park, known as the "flopper." The opinion of the court in denying recovery to the plaintiff on the ground of assumption of the risk is particularly apt to officials:

One who takes part in such a sport accepts the dangers that inhere in it insofar as they are obvious and necessary, just as a fencer accepts the risk of a thrust by his antagonist, or a spectator at a ball game the chance of contact with the ball. The antics of the clown are not the poses of the cloistered cleric. The rough and boisterous joke, the horseplay of the crowd, evokes its own guffaws, but they are not the pleasures of tranquility. The plaintiff was not seeking a retreat for meditation . . . . The timorous may stay at home. (250 N.Y., at 482-3, 166 N.e. at 174-75 (citations omitted).

You'll recall from "The Liability Trap," that more than one person or entity may be liable under the law to compensate an injured plaintiff. This, of course, is no less true in situations where officials are injured than where players are injured. However, the official has a formidable task to prove liability on the part of competing institutions or the sponsoring league in the event that the official is assaulted during or after a game.

Consider, for example, the following situation: Imagine you're a minor league baseball umpire working the bases before a crowd of 3,400. Imagine further that you have a couple of tough calls and they both go against the home team. Then, picture yourself being challenged on both calls by the home team manager, who tells you that if you make one more adverse decision, he will behave in such a manner that you will have to eject him and the crowd will be riled up and hostile towards you after that.

To make things worse, suppose that there was another adverse decision, this time in the 9th inning, against the home team. Imagine the manager coming out cursing you and refusing to control his players who were pushing and shoving you. Imagine ejecting this manager from the game and then imagine him continuing to stay on the field for 10 minutes or so while advising you that you would receive no help from him or his players in getting off the field.

If you could then imagine yourself being struck on the head by one of his 3400 fans in attendance and severely injured, you'd have a situation very similar to the one mentioned in the famous case of *Toone v. Adams*[2], which arose out of a game between the Greensboro Yankees and the Raleigh Caps in the Carolina League on June 16, 1960.

When the smoke cleared, the umpire sued his attacker, the manager and the team. The allegations against the manager and the team were that there was a duty to avoid the conduct which would incite the fans to assault the plaintiff, and also there was a duty to protect the umpire while he left the field at the conclusion of the game. The Supreme Court of North Carolina ruled that the lack of police protection for the plaintiff was not one of the proximate causes of injury. The court pointed out that two policemen and the plaintiff's fellow umpire were escorting him and that the assault was at the hands of one spectator out of 3,452 in attendance.

Further, the court held that the manager's unsportsmanlike conduct was removed from the assault in terms of time, and that the manager knew nothing of the fan's intent to assault the umpire, ruling that to say the manager's conduct was the proximate cause of the attack was too speculative. The court concluded that:

> It would be an intolerable burden upon managers of baseball teams to saddle them with responsibility for the actions of every emotionally unstable person who might arrive at the game spoilng for a fight and become enraged over an umpire's call which the manager had protested.

The fallacies in the reasoning notwithstanding, it's still interesting to note that there was no question that the person who attacked the umpire is liable under the law for his actions; however, the other acts of the team personnel, though unsportsmanlike and perhaps negligent, were not sufficient grounds, at least in the opinion of one court, to sustain liability against either the manager or the team. All this is not to say that recovery may never be available to you as against a school board, league or other institution if inadequate or nonexistent security, coupled with a flagrant abuse of sportsmanship on the part of team personnel is adjudged to be the proximate cause of your injury. Undoubtedly, there will be more of this type of litigation in the future as reports of violence against game officials escalate.

But what about the purely *accidental* injury suffered by an official? Take "the case of the flying bat ring." In *Stewart v. D & R Welding Supply Co.*,[3] the injury occurred between innings of a softball game. The first batter was taking practice swings with a weighted bat ring affixed to his bat. The ring apparently was the wrong size for the bat and flew off the end, striking the plaintiff, the plate umpire.

The Appellate Court of Illinois held that a player owes the same duty of care to an umpire as he would owe to another player during a game. Citing an earlier case, the court adopted the position that a reckless disregard of safety of players and officials could be the basis of a lawsuit.

As you can see, given the present state of the law, it is fairly difficult under most circumstances for an official to recover his medical expenses and compensation for pain and suffering and lost wages, etc., if he is unintentionally injured while officiating.

There is, however, another system for compensating injured persons, separate and apart from the third party or "fault" system of litigation. All states in the United States have statutes governing compensation for victims of injuries occurring on the job. This is known as *worker's compensation,* and is a so-called no-fault system, meaning that neither negligence nor any other actionable legal event is necessary for an injured employee to receive compensation. All that is necessary is that the injured party be an employee, as opposed to an independent contractor, and that the injury arises out of and in the course of the employment.

This is another instance of where the distinction between employee and independent contractor as it relates to game officials is often blurred and fraught with much doubt. As mentioned before, officials working in different situations may argue that they are accorded one status or the other for one purpose or another. Unfortunately, the reported case law on the topic has been unfavorable to the official from the point of view that recovery has been denied in the reported cases. However, this is not to say that officials have not brought actions claiming status as an employee for the purposes of workers' compensation and had favorable results or settled matters favorably prior to final resolution.

Workers' compensation is a significant issue for not only individual officials, but also for associations of officials, who have in the past been accused of being employers of officials for purposes of workers' compensation law. This is one situation where an individual official may well be in conflict with his association. For a further discussion see the chapter entitled "Officials Associations."

Three reported cases on the subject all came down with the same result. In *Daniels v. Gates Rubber Company, et al.*[4], a softball umpire brought an action in the workers' compensation forum against the company that sponsored softball games for their employees and others, but also against the umpire's association. The claim against the umpire's association was ultimately dismissed, and there was no appeal. However, the corporation that sponsored the league was found to be liable under the workers' compensation laws of the State of Colorado. An appeal was taken from this decision, and the Colorado Court of Appeals decided the matter against the umpire.

In the Maryland case of *Gale v. Greater Washington Softball Umpires' Association*[5], a softball umpire sought workers' compensation when, in the words of the Court of Special Appeals for the State of Maryland, a player

> ... attempted to persuade the umpire that the call was missed, and presented his point of view rather forcefully by striking Gale about the neck, hip and legs with a baseball bat, temporarily incapacitating him.

Gale proceeded to file a complaint with the Maryland Workman's Compensation Commission, which ruled that Gale was an independent contractor and thus not entitled to workers' compensation benefits. The Court of Special Appeals upheld this ruling on appeal and ruled that the umpire was not an employee of the Softball Umpires' Association. Although the Umpires' Association collected the game fees from the leagues they serviced and disbursed game fees to the umpires, as well as having a commissioner who assigned the games, the workers' compensation judge found that umpires were free to accept or reject assignments and conduct their games without any supervision of the association during the game.

A third and most recent of reported cases was the New Jersey case of *Ehehalt v. Livingston Board of Education*.[6] In this 1977 case, the plaintiff basketball official was struck in the mouth by an errant basketball. Here, the official claimed workers' compensation benefits to be due from the school board which hired him to officiate the game. Once again, the court, this time the Appellate Division of the Superior Court of New Jersey, ruled that the official, who worked at various schools, was an independent contractor and not an employee of the school that hired him, for purposes of workers' compensation law.

11

OFFICIALS' ASSOCIATIONS

Officials' associations vary widely in the degree of control and supervision that they exercise with respect to their members. A comprehensive study of officials' groups could fill a volume larger than this. Clearly, though, all associations in one way or another have certain items in common. First, they are promulgators of information. They pass information about the rules and interpretations and, hopefully, mechanics, on to their members. Whether this is done simply through buying books such as rule books, case books and officials' manuals and distributing them to members; or whether they have a complex series of clinics throughout the season, all officials' associations are in the business of distributing information. One association of baseball umpires meets every Monday night, with a three week break for Christmas, throughout the year!

Secondly, many associations serve as assignment bureaus. That is to say, through one or more individuals, the association is directly responsible for the who, what, when, and where of the officials' officiating. This type of association actually assigns the official his games.

Needless to say, coupled with this function is the function of deciding who works where and when. These types of activities present difficulties for an association far beyond those faced by the association, which is primarily a conduit for information. Both functions are of course fundamental to the official's existence and can greatly influence his or her success.

Then, again, some officials work through no association. This was somewhat of a surprise to me in speaking with some officials from Western states, where, apparently, associations of officials are less common than they are in the East. Superimposed on this structure is the specter of the State High School Interscholastic Athletic Association.

For college officials, in most cases, the college conference with which they become associated is their official association. That is to say, the conference distributes the information in the form of rule books, manuals and other materials to them, supervises their officiating activities, makes their assignments and in general governs their conduct concerning the college sport involved. In other areas, conferences contract with an association of officials who elect their own officers, have their own by-laws and regulations, and discipline their own members, but the college conference itself distributes information, makes the assignments, and sets forth standards to be followed by the officials.

Much has been spoken in recent years about the desirability of incorporating officials' associations. The single most compelling factor in a decision to incorporate is the shield that incorporation offers from personal liability in the event of a lawsuit against the association.

Let's take a quick look at the difference between unincorporated associations and associations which have chosen the corporate form (called in most states "not-for-profit" corporations). Although state laws governing unincorporated associations vary, the general rule is that each and every member of an unincorporated association may be liable for the entire amount of damages assessed against his association in a legal proceeding. The exposure to members and officers of unincorporated associations can range from liability on a debt of the association to the printer of the rosters, or the banquet hall, or a parent organization should the funds with which to pay this indebtedness be mislaid, or misappropriated, to liability on a multi-million dollar lawsuit brought by an injured player or spectator. Although there are different ways to assess this liability in terms of calling upon each member individually to participate, the point remains that there is an exposure for members and officers of officials' associations which are not incorporated far beyond that of members of associations who have become corporations.

Be careful, though, not to assume that incorporating your local association will automatically and completely absolve members and/or officers from personal liability in all circumstances and under all conditions. This is not the case. The situations which may give rise to personal liability, especially on the part of officers and directors of corporations, fall under a certain classification of actions known as *ultra vires*. This, loosely translated, means outside the scope of the actions of a corporation.

Still, an officials' association which does incorporate becomes, in the eyes of the law, a legal "person." That is to say, it has its own existence and, generally speaking, is liable for its debts, obligations, torts and contracts, aside from any liability of members. Therefore, if those the association are dealing with who use the services of, or deal with the Anytown Wrestling Officials Association Incorporated, a not-for-profit corporation, members individually will not be liable for obligations or acts or omissions of that corporate entity.

Of course, as in all things in life, with the benefits of incorporation are coupled corresponding responsibilities for those associations undertaking this step.

Generally speaking, corporations are regulated somewhat more closely than unincorporated associations by governmental authorities. A corporation, being a legal person, has not only rights but responsibilities and obligations under the law, separate and distinct from those of its members and/or officers.

The officers and directors of a corporation are charged with responsibility of fulfilling those obligations. These include maintaining appropriate bank accounts, records of activities of the association and filing reports where necessary. Insurance coverage should be maintained in the name of the association to protect the corporate assets and property. Moreover, the directors of a corporation, and officers, have a fiduciary duty to the corporation. This means that those charged with administering the operation of the corporation must do so in a reasonably prudent manner with a view toward preserving the assets of the corporation and carrying out the functions for which the organization was organized, in a fashion which is reasonably calculated not to waste or dissipate the corporation's assets, to the detriment of the members. For, transgressions involving breaches or violations of fiduciary duty, directors and officers may indeed be personally liable.

If your local association is not incorporated, now is definitely the time to consult with your association attorney about the advisability of taking the plunge into incorporation. The cost is nominal, both in terms of legal fees and filing fees to the state so cost is not a factor. Along with incorporation will come a review by your association attorney of your constitution and/or by-laws to bring them in line with state laws, if necessary, and make any other changes, additions or deletions which would best serve the interests of the members of the new corporation.

A word about executive committees. Surely there are almost as many different names or terms for the governing bodies of officials' associations as there are states in the Union. I've heard these groups referred to as executive committees, board of directors, board of trustees, executive board, officers committee, or board of directors, and a smaller executive committee, made up of some of the members of the board of directors. This is true usually of organizations which cover a wide geographical area, making it difficult to assemble a complete board of directors to take action or transact business.

Additionally, there are varied methods of stocking this pond of governing bodies. Some boards are elected directly by the membership. Some appointed by the president, and some chosen by other methods. One officials' organization rotates directorships amongst the entire active membership. This last case is the exception rather than the rule. In most associations, directors and officers are elected or nominated by a nominating committee which presents a slate of officers for consideration by members. Nominations are usually permitted from the floor, and sometimes by write-ins, so that competitive elections can and often do occur.

In larger associations, there is often a geographical basis of qualification of election or nomination to office and staggered terms, similar to the United States congressional system, are often used. The geographical basis for election is, of course, to assure that members residing in various geographical areas under the association's jurisdiction be represented and thus have a voice in the operation and governance of the association. The staggering of terms so just a portion of directors are elected each term ensures that any given board of directors at any time will have veteran directors serving so as to guide and give continuity to the affairs of the association. In any event, these are matters to be included in your association by-laws.

Many unincorporated officials' associations have two sets of regulations. These are called constitution and by-laws. The reason for having both a constitution and by-laws is that the constitution was traditionally reserved for matters fundamental and basic to the organization that are not frequently changed (or, when they are changed, require specific previous notice to the members and the vote of a large majority). By-laws were traditionally reserved for matters which change more often, such as the details of amount of dues, frequency of meetings, etc. These are easier to amend than constitutional provisions, and thus the reason for two separate instruments.

The modern approach has been to combine these documents into one instrument. This instrument may be called either constitution or by-laws or constitution and by-laws.

It is necessary to have your constitution or by-laws refer to a more detailed authority on procedure for conduct of meetings, especially where a dispute arises between members as to the procedure to be employed or as to whether or not to take up that piece of business. Most organizations use the old (1876) master, *Robert's Rules of Order* as their authority where by-laws do not otherwise specify. General Henry M. Robert's classic work is the foundation upon which all modern parliamentary procedure, more or less, is based. *Robert's Rules of Order,* in all its editions, has sold about 2.7 million copies.

General Robert died in 1923. The work has been revised in what many have called a less-than-successful attempt to keep up with current mores and practice. Nonetheless, it remains a difficult and obtuse treatise. And, there is probably more misinformation floating around about a particular point than there is about the infield fly rule or the convoluted lack of action procedure in basketball.

Be that as it may, *Robert's* remains the leader. If your by-laws cite *Robert's Rules,* or any recognized text, and action is taken on a procedural point based upon or with reference to those rules, in the event of a member challenging the association's decision, the court may look to the text to ensure that business was conducted correctly.

Other comprehensive and well prepared manuals of parliamentary procedure have come along in recent years, including *Demeter's,* and the American Bar Association-American Law Institute Model Parliamentary Rules for Non-Profit Organizations. They are listed in the bibliography and certainly worth looking into if you are contemplating a change or forming a new organization. The American Bar Association-American Law Institute Model Parliamentary Rules for Non-Profit Organizations rules are particularly suited to today's not-for-profit organizations. They're streamlined, relatively easy to read and digest, and provide guidance for many of the practical problems of today's associations where the by-laws leave off.

Keep in mind that no set of by-laws can possibly cover *every* situation which will confront your association. Indeed, a document that would propose to cover in great detail all questions revolving around the members' relationship to the association would be so unwieldly that probably no one would ever pick it up and look at it. Therefore, you must, with your attorney, look at the way your association functions, the kind of activities in which it participates, the number of members, and the type of contact that the association maintains with the members, as well as the degree of dominion the association exercises with respect to members officiating. Then, you must look at the situations which tend to surface in the context of your association's day-to-day activities.

Does your association assign members to games or matches? Does your association have different "sub-groups" or "satellites"? Does your association prescribe strict standards of dress and conduct for its officials? Does your association have attendance, testing and certification requirements? Does your association have various classes of membership? How large a geographical area does your association cover? Does your association supply officials or have jurisdiction over a particular type of competition (i.e., college only, high school only, a mixture of interscholastic and independent leagues, etc.)?

The answers to all of these questions and more are necessary if your attorney is to be able to adequately prepare by-laws which will well serve your group.

Minutes of meetings should be kept by all associations and should be kept for not only regular association meetings, but all meetings of committees and boards of directors. In the case of incorporated associations, minutes are often required by state law to be kept and attested to by an officer, usually the secretary, as being accurate minutes of what transpired. Secretaries should note that minutes of any meeting should ideally record what was *done* and *not* what was said.

Many association secretaries, in an effort to be conscientious and accurately report what transpired in a given meeting, recite in great detail the blow by blow of debates on various items of business presented to the body. Not only does this use a lot of paper and ink, but it is usually a gratuitous exercise and clouds the important aspect of the minutes, i.e., reflecting action taken by the group. In executive committee deliberations, there will be differences of opinion from time to time. Debate must flow freely if the association is to elect the best alternative for a given course of action. If all the give and take of debate were to be recounted in minutes open to inspection by the membership, or perhaps by those outside the membership, under certain circumstances, the members of a board or executive committee may not so freely set forth arguments on one side or the other of a controversial issue.

Oftentimes difficulties arise with respect to an association attempting to impose disciplinary sanctions on one of its officials. This is an area where officials associations occasionally end up in court, forced to defend their actions under the scrutiny of the law. This need not be the case. If certain precautions are followed, there is no reason why an officials' association cannot exercise legitimate sanctions against members who violate its by-laws.

Although, traditionally, courts have been reluctant to interfere in the affairs of private associations, members of any association, by reason of their membership, are said to have a contract with the an officials' association, he makes a pact to abide by its rules. If either the association or the member violates this fact, legal consequences may ensue.

There are three factors which render officials' associations particularly susceptible to having a court review their actions with respect to discipline of members:

- in many areas membership in a particular officials' association is a prerequisite to officiating engagements, which pay money;
- most officials' associations are dealing with public entities, such as schools and local recreation departments and, as such, in these areas, courts are more likely to take an interest than they would in the event of a member being expelled from the local Elks Club;

- official's associations typically do not spell out what is expected of members with appropriate by-laws or policy documents so the official is not apprised, in advance, of what activities may be frowned upon.

All this being said, officials' associations, being essentially private entities, are entirely free to impose sanctions on members, so long as procedural safeguards are employed so a member will not be unfairly or arbitrarily treated. Common sense really paves the way here. Legal requirements are quite simple and, if followed, an association should have no difficulty in maintaining its policies with respect to discipline of members.

Basically, a member of an officials' association has a right to know what is expected of him and what types of activities are prohibited. If an association chooses to enact detailed by-law provisions regarding conduct while officiating and requirements for officials to maintain their membership, that is all well and good. If an officials' association wants to prescribe a particular manual as a guideline for its members, this too is entirely satisfactory, so long as it is spelled out.

Having been apprised, then, of what is expected of him, should an official stray from the fold and violate his association's by-laws, the next step is the critical one. It's simply good common sense to know that a mere accusation by one person against another person does not make the accusation true. Therefore, if there is a complaint that a member has booked 4 games on the same date and showed up for none, or struck the goalkeeper's grandmother in the mouth after a hotly disputed penalty kick, the accused member must have the opportunity to defend himself! This is known in legal circles as due process. In other words, simply because an accusation is made, officials' associations must not go from an accusation to presuming that the accusation is true. Rather, your association by-laws should provide that a member accused be given a hearing. If any penalty is involved, ranging from a fine to suspension or expulsion, or to a pulling of a schedule, the member must have an opportunity to confront his accuser. He must be able to cross-examine his accuser and make any statements in his own behalf and present evidence and testimony in his own behalf to refute the accusations against him. There is no one correct procedure for all associations and all circumstances. But, the basic concept of notice of the charges and fair hearing is an absolute requirement if the procedure is to be sustained if challenged in court.

Finally, there should be an appeal procedure in the event that, after hearing, the member is adjudged to have been guilty of the offense charged and then disciplined. Many associations provide that a disciplinary hearing be held before the executive committee and the *appeal* procedure, if desired, could go before the entire membership. As we said before, common sense goes a long way in these matters.

Common sense goes a long way during disciplinary hearings.

WORKER'S COMPENSATION AND OTHER THINGS

In Chapter 10, we learned about several litigated cases which involved an official bringing a claim against his association for injuries sustained while officiating, alleging that the official was in fact an employee of his officials' association and thus entitled to workers' compensation. In these cases, the courts have decided that the official was *not* an employee, for purposes of workers' compensation, of his officials' association. However, this is not to say that the day will not come when claims by officials against their officials' association in the workers' compensation courts will not be sustained. Aside from the high cost of workers' compensation insurance, the concept of an official being an employee of his own association can lead to severe legal consequences.

Employers are subject to a wide variety of state, and sometimes federal, regulations concerning their relationship with their employees. All officials should raise serious questions as to whether it is desirable for an association of officials to participate in activities which might lead a court to the conclusion that such an association is an *employer* of officials. The traditional view is that officials function as independent contractors for the schools or leagues who hire them. Since the officials' associations are formulated principally to aid the official in training, protection, and securing assignments, it is generally not to an official's advantage to foment an employer-employee relationship with an association of officials. Even such mundane matters as income taxes can spell large scale headaches for officials in certain organizations when the question of their status arises.

The Internal Revenue Service was asked on at least two occasions to rule on questions of whether or not athletic officials are employees or independent contractors. In 1957, a college conference requested a ruling from the IRS, stating that the conference by-laws authorized the selection, training and assignment of officials for all intercollegiate contests, and mandatory conduct of officiating clinics. The conference also indicated that they require their officials to make a report to the association after each game. Beyond that, the conference had the power to terminate the services of officials at any time during the season. Under these circumstances, the Internal Revenue Service ruled that there did exist an employer-employee relationship and therefore required federal withholding tax to be taken from game fees.[1]

Some ten years later, a similar question was asked by an association of high school officials. This association also assigned members to officiate games and conducted clinics. One difference was that, according to the IRS statement of facts, the official had the option of accepting or rejecting an offer to officiate at a particular school. In this case, the IRS ruled that the officials were not employees for purposes of federal income taxation.[2]

In short, you will want to do what you can to negate the inference that your association is an employer of officials.

If you do not work under the assigner or commissioner system, this is strong evidence that your association is not an employer. If you do use an assigner, make sure that the officials are paid directly by the schools or league. Don't permit your association to function as a conduit for game fees.

THE GREAT CONTRACT MYTH

For most people, officials included, the word, contract, signifies a printed document, often written in language that is hard to understand, with lines for the signatures of the parties to the contract. Accompanying this image of a contract as a written instrument is the essentially negative connotation of the word contract. The old joke among lawyers is; if you don't want someone to sign something, call it a contract. If you do want someone to sign something, call it an agreement.

Like the proverbial rose, a contract by any other name, or form, for that matter, smells the same. The prevalent misconception among officials and athletic directors alike is that a contract must be written to be valid. This is simply not true. An oral contract is every bit as valid and enforceable as a written contract. The difficulty comes in proving the terms and existence of an oral contract, when there is nothing tangible to present. With certain exceptions, oral contracts are enforceable just as if each and every term had been written and a document signed by the parties.

What's important for you to remember is that contracts in writing are easier to prove and, naturally, the more items that are spelled out in the writing the less there will be for a third party to determine in the event of a dispute. In the same fashion that the rules of a sport must be sufficiently broad to cover most items that may arise, the terms of a contract should cover most of the common contingencies that may occur. These are basically the fee, date, time of cancellation, rain-out arrangements, number of officials on the game and working conditions. To the extent that any of these items are not covered, in the event that someone has to decide whether or not the contract was violated, it will be necessary to look to the custom of the parties, that is to say, how they have dealt in the past with similar situations.

All things considered, then, it's far preferable to have written confirmation of your officiating engagements. At the same time, keep in mind that your verbal agreement to officiate will often be legally and always ethically binding on you.

WHY YOUR ASSOCIATION NEEDS TO FOLLOW A CODE OF ETHICS

If you asked a hundred referees or umpires what was the least read segment of any officials' manual, I'd be willing to bet it's that pompous sounding squib at the end of the manual bearing such a lofty title as "A Code of Ethics for Athletic Officials," or "the Athletic Official's Creed."

Dismissed by most every working official as impractical and verbose, the code of ethics included in the literature for officials, when you get down to it, doesn't quite deserve its bad reputation. If one didn't get the sense that ethics codes were handed down from on high by some theoretician totally devoid of practical experience, perhaps more attention might be paid to them. As it is, the attitude of most officials on the subject of ethics, and it is an attitude not without some justification, is that the system here just doesn't work that way.

Is a code of ethics important for officials? I'd like to convince you that the answer to this question is a resounding yes. Think about this; as officials, ethics is our bag! Or, what is ethics if it isn't fair play and a notion of "good for the goose and good for the gander" in practice. Isn't our entire function, once we step onto the field, pitch court, or mat, to see that the best team that day wins? Isn't our entire function based upon the notion that someone must take the responsibility for conducting the competition according to rule? When the media and losing coach get together after a tough game, sometimes a peculiar view of the ethics of sport is raised.

You recognize the scene: two major college basketball teams from the east are engaged in the traditional "barn burner." The Hangtough University (visiting) team travelled 200 miles to play in the Alibi University (home) team's always-filled-to-capacity, on-campus field house. The home team builds a 6-point lead with a minute and a half left in the game. Somehow or other, Hangtough University pulls it out of the fire and comes away with a 1-point victory.

Predictably, Larry Sportswriter, the local journalist, who covers Alibi all year, gives an "expert" analysis of the game. After allowing for the fact that Alibi scored one basket in the final minute and a half, Larry Sportswriter sets the stage for a notable quote from the Alibi coach, always one to take responsibility in good times or bad:

"Frustrating is losing at home on some questionable calls. 'We might as well have played at Hangtough,' said the Coach of Alibi. 'We're a North Paducah team and we get South Paducah refs in crucial games.'"

What did he mean by saying they're a team from one state and they get referees from a neighboring state in a crucial game? Did he mean that the officials who happen to live in the state where Alibi University was located would do other than call an honest game? Did he mean that the officials who happen to reside in the state where Alibi

University is located would cheat in favor of the home team? Did he mean that it would take a referee from another state to be fair? It may be ugly, but that, folks, is what separates us from them.

The story wouldn't be complete without a follow-up from our friends at the sports department of the local newspaper. A year or two later, when this well renowned coach announced that he was hanging up his sweatsuit in order to enter the private sector, an enterprising reporter, not the same one who offered the analysis of the loss to Hangtough, came to this pillar of the community for some appropriate words, as he put it, to pose the question, "What advice would he give a young coach?"

The response was "Marry the right girl. Don't mind the long hours. Enjoy the report and camaraderie of the players and your fellow coaches. Realize that from one of the last real realms of authority you can reconstruct or further the values of the home. You can help make a kid a better person."

We have no way of knowing, of course, what "values of the home" our righteous friend was referring to. But, we can assume that integrity and ethics are not on his list.

As for our list, as officials, isn't ethics high on the list? Doesn't ethics separate us from the ignorance of the media and the hypocracy of administrators who proclaim the "values of the home" while publicly castigating us as officials for calling an honest game?

12

THE LAST CALL

Officiating sports is a challenge, perhaps a bigger challenge than at any time in the past.

It's virtually impossible to be a sports official today and not be touched by the legal system in some fashion.

Undoubtedly, the fact that athletes have come to realize that their legal rights do not end at the stadium gate has made it a necessity that the official be aware of the legal issues that confront him every time he goes out to work. Officials, too, must be able to use the legal system to preserve and protect their rights, especially in this era of increasing violent assaults on officials of all sports.

As we have indicated, some of the principles of law discussed in this book may not apply in your state or locality. Sports officials, however, are experiencing increased contacts with the legal system in *every* locality. Hopefully, what you have read in these pages will inspire you to keep one ear tuned in to the all important factor of player safety, no matter what sport you're working.

Further, the suggestions in this book are intended to aid you should you have the desire or the need to assert your rights in a legal forum.

For, when we appreciate both the extent of our legal responsibilities and the measure of protection the law affords us, officiating sports will be a better game for all of us.

FOOTNOTES

Notes to Chapter 3
1. Carabba v. The Anacortes School District No. 102, et als, 436 P. 2nd 936 (Washington, 1967).
2. Pantalone v. Lenape Valley Regional School District, Superior Court of New Jersey, Docket No. L-40828-76.

Notes to Chapter 4
1. Drs. Gerberich and Priest, paper published at University of Notre Dame, forwarded by Leslie M. Bodnar, M.D.

Notes to Chapter 5
1. Hinton v. Pateros School District No. 122, et als., No. 29847 Supp. Ct. Wash. (County of Chelan, 1976).

Notes to Chapter 9
1. Stock v. Texas Catholic Interscholastic League, 364 F. Supp. 362, 1972.
2. New York Times Co. v. Sullivan, 376 U.S. 254, 11 L E d 2nd 686, 84 S Ct. 710 (SupremeCourt 1964); Gertz v. Robert Welch, Inc., 418 U. S. 323, 41 L E d 2nd 789, 94 S. Ct. 2997 (Supreme Court, 1974).

Notes to Chapter 10
1. Murphy v. Steeplechase Amusement Co., 50 N.Y. 479, 166 N.E. 173 (Ct. of Appeals of New York, 1929).
2. 137 S.E. 2nd 132 (No. Carolina, 1964).
3. 366 N.E. 2nd 1107 (Ill., 1977).
4. 479 P. 2nd 983 (1970).
5. 311 A. 2nd 817 (1973).
6. N.J. Super, Appellate Division, (1977).

Notes to Chapter 11
1. Revenue Ruling 57-119, Internal Revenue Service.
2. Revenue Ruling 67-119, Internal Revenue Service.

SELECTED BIBLIOGRAPHY

Appenzeller, Herb. *Athletics and The Law,* The Michie Company, 1975

Appenzeller, Herb. *From the Gym to the Jury,* The Michie Company, 1970

Appenzeller, Herb. *Physical Education and the Law,* The Michie Company, 1978

Appenzeller, Herb and Appenzeller, Thomas. *Sports and the Courts,* The Michie Company, 1980

Atyeo, Don. *Violence in Sports,* Van Nostrand Reinhold Company, 1981

Bunn, John W. *The Art of Officiating Sports,* New Jersey: Prentice-Hall, Inc., 1957

Decof, Leonard and Godosky, Richard. *Sports Injury Litigation, Practicing Law Institute, 1979*

Clegg, R. and Thompson, W.A. *Modern Sports Officiating: A Practical Guide,* Dubuque, Iowa: William C. Brown Company, 1974

Demeter, George. *Demeter's Manual of Parliamentary Law and Procedure,* Mass.: Little, Brown and Company, 1969

Dolan, Edward F., Jr. *Calling the Play,* Antheneum, 1981

Eskenazi, Gerald. *A Thinking Man's Guide to Pro Soccer,* E.P. Dutton, 1980

Franklin, Marc A. *Injuries and Remedies, Cases and Materials on Tort Law and Alternatives,* New York: The Foundation Press, Inc., 1971

Gallner, Sheldon M. *Pro Sports: The Contract Game,* New York: Charles Scribner's Sons, 1974

Geriach, Larry R. *The Men in Blue: Conversations With Umpires,* New York; The Viking Press, 1980

Gorman, Tom. as told to Holtzman, Jerome. *Three and Two,* New York: Charles Scribner's Sons, 1979

Gutkind, Lee. *The Best Seat in Baseball, But You Have to Stand,* The Dial Press, 1975

Handbook of the International Association of Approved Basketball Officials, Inc., 1982-1983, International Association of Approved Basketball Officials, Inc.

Kahn, James M. *The Umpire Story,* New York: G.P. Putnam's Sons, 1953

Kovalakides, Nick. *Official's Manual: Soccer,* West Point, New York: Leisure Press, 1978

Lever, Janet. *Soccer Madness,* The University of Chicago Press, 1983

Lipsky, Richard. *How We Play the Game,* Boston; Beacon Press, 1981

Markbriet, Jerry. *The Armchair Referee,* Garden City, New York: Doubleday & Company, Inc., 1973

McDonough, John with Owens, Paul T., *Don't Hit Him, He's Dead, Celestial Arts, 1978*

Miller, Gary L. *Official's Manual: Basketball,* West Point, New York: Leisure Press, 1981

Mitchell, Elmer D. *Sports Officiating,* New York: The Ronald Press Company, Inc., 1949

National Collegiate Athletic Association, *NCAA Manual,* Kansas: The National Collegiate Athletic Association, 1980

NCAA. *1982 NCAA Baseball, NCAA, 1981*

National Association for Girls & Women in Sport Basketball, American Alliance For Health, Physical Education, Recreation and Dance, 1983

1983 NCAA Men's Basketball Rules and Interpretations, National Collegiate Athletic Association, 1982

NCAA. *NCAA Football Rules and Interpretations,* NCAA, 1981

1983 NCAA Man's Soccer Rules, National Collegiate Athletic Association, 1983

1983 NCAA Wrestling Rules, National Collegiate Athletic Association, 1982

1983 Official High School Baseball Case Book, The National Federation of State High School Associations, 1983

1983 and 1984 Official High School Football Handbook, National Federation of State High School Associations, 1983

The National Federation of State High School Associations, Football Case Book, National Federation of State High School Associations, 1983

The National Federation of State High School Associations, Football Rule Book, National Federation of State High School Associations, 1983

1982-1983 Soccer Rule Book, The National Federation of State High School Associations, 1982

1983 Official High School Softball Rule Book, The National Federation of State High School Associations, 1983

1982/83 & 1983/84 Official Federation of State High School Associations, 1982

1982/83 Official High School Wrestling Rules, National Federation of State High School Associations, 1982

Oleck, Howard L. *Non-Profit Corporation, Organization, and Association,* Third Edition, New Jersey: Prentice-Hall, Inc., 1974

Oleck, Howard L. *Parliamentary Law for Nonprofit Organizations,* American Law Institute, 1979

Oleck, Howard L. *Trends in Nonprofit Organization Law,* The American Law Institute, 1977

Powers, Richie with Mulvoy, Mark. *Overtime,* New York: Ballantine Books, 1975

Ralbovsky, Martin. *Lords of the Locker Room,* New York: Peter H. Wyden, 1974

Rittler, Kathy. *Official's Manual: Softball,* West Point, New York, 1982

Robert, Henry M., III. *The Scott, Foresman Robert's Rules of Order Newly Revised,* Illinois: Scott, Foresman and Company, 1981

Sobel, Lionel S. *Professional Sports & The Law,* Arts Publishers, Inc., 1977

Sturgis, Alice. *Sturgis Standard Code of Parliamentary Procedure,* McGraw-Hill Book Company , 1966

Underwood, John. *The Death of an American Game,* The Crisis in Football, Little, Brown and Company, 1979

Weistart, John C. and Lowell, Cym H. *The Law of Sports,* The Dobbs-Merrill Company, Inc., 1979

Williams, Jesse, Feiring and Brownell, Clifford Lee. *The Administration of Health and Physical Education-Second Edition,* W.B. Saunders Company, 1940

Yeager, Robert C. *Seasons of Shame, The New Violence in Sports,* McGraw-Hill Book Company, 1979

APPENDIX A

IMPROVING THE EDUCATIONAL VALUES OF INTERSCHOLASTIC ATHLETICS BY PROVIDING FOR BETTER SPORTSMANSHIP AND CONDUCT.

Providing for Better Sportsmanship and Conduct

Introduction

Interscholastic athletic games have been sponsored by the high schools because of their belief that they have both educational and recreational values for high school students which are significantly worthwhile to include interschool games in the school program. Games have been considered a diversion from curricular studies for high school students and a recreational pastime for student and adult fans.

Approximately two-thirds of the member schools have received no reports from officials for unsportsmanlike conduct of players, coaches, or fans, which indicates that they are providing a wholesome and worthwhile program for their students and school communities. The Board of Control sincerely commends these schools for their efforts.

Increasing instances of unsportsmanlike conduct, however, have caused many to question whether these activities are continuing to provide educational and recreational values. Although teaching students to compete has been considered both educationally sound and desirable in a competitive society, an obsession for winning which has developed has, in the opinion of many educators and athletic administrators, caused a loss of sight of the educational and recreational values of interscholastic competition. Debates regarding overemphasis on competition have been confusing. It is educationally sound and worthwhile to teach an individual to do his or her best at any undertaking, whether it be in the classroom or on the ath-

---

*Reprinted with the kind permission of Mr. Jack Miles of the Missouri State High School Activities Association.

letic field, but when the person becomes so obsessed with winning that he or she loses site of the educational and recreational values of competition, winning is without question being overemphasized. This overemphasis on winning is the primary cause of most of the unsportsmanlike conduct and misconduct which has occurred at athletic games.

Schools must take definite steps to provide for better sportsmanship and conduct at interscholastic games, or interscholastic athletics may well lose both their educational and recreational values. The MSHSAA Board of Control is providing recommendations in this manual to aid its member schools in providing the type of sportsmanship that will enhance the educational values of interscholastics. It may well be used as a guide in evaluating plans for the school's interscholastic athletic program and will provide the basis for the Board of Control's consideration of reports of unsportsmanlike conduct.

Board of Education

The board of education is responsible to the school community for giving direction to the interscholastic program as it is for all other phases of the school program. In assuming this school responsibility, it is recommended that it:

- Adopt a philosophy and objectives for interscholastics. A statement of such should be developed by school administrators and presented to the board of education for its approval.
- Approve policies to implement the school's philosophy and objectives. These should be recommended to the board of education by administrative officers for its approval.

The *MSHSAA Interscholastic Activities Manual for Boards of Education,* pages 6-7, is suggested as a basis for this consideration.

High School Administrator

The high school principal must assume the responsibility of leadership in guiding the interscholastic athletic program of the school. He or she may delegate authority and responsibility to an athletic director and other persons on the staff. However, the principal will be the one who is held responsible to the board of education and superintendent of schools. In assuming his or her responsibilities the following are recommended:

- The development of a recommended statement of philosophy and objectives for the school program to submit to the superintendent and board of education for approval. The principal may appoint a committee to formulate such a statement, or may do it in consultation with staff members and students. The basic principles and statements of philosophy and objectives found on pages 3-5 of the *MSHSAA Student Activities Manual* will provide aids to the person, or person, who assumes this responsibility.

- Policies to implement the school's philosophy and to attain its objectives must be formulated and presented to the superintendent and board of education for approval. These will include administrative policies, standards of sportsmanship and procedures to be applied when violations occur. The *MSHSAA Recommended Guide for Athletic Contest Management Details* will be helpful in consideration of policies.
- Adequate game supervision shall be provided. Faculty members should be assigned as supervisors who will report both problems and potential problems to the administrator in charge and to law enforcement officers when necessary. Arrangements should be made for adequate police protection, but their efforts should be to supplement those of the school rather than to replace any responsibility of the school. School representatives and police should keep students and adult spectators off the playing floor or field after games are concluded. Spectators should not be permitted to gather at the sidelines or endlines of the playing area while a game is in progress.
- Procedure for handling gross misconduct cases should be developed. Attacks upon officials, fans, etc., should be handled under legal procedures. Charges may be brought or information may be reported to the prosecuting attorney who can file charges under Missouri law without identifying the person providing him with information. Recommendations contained in the article, *The Supportive People in Crowd Control,* found on pages 29-32 of the AAHPER Manual, *Crowd Control for High School Athletics,* will be very helpful in providing for proper supervision and in delegating responsibilities for such. (This manual is available through the MSHSAA Office at a reduced price of $1.50.)

Athletic Coach
The athletic coach in his or her strategic position is the most influential person upon the sportsmanship and conduct of players and spectators. Hence, the coach shall be expected to assume the following responsibilities:
- To set a proper example. The coach shall maintain a professional attitude toward fellow coaches and toward athletic game officials. Complaints should be filed through the proper channel, and he (she) should avoid showing any disrespect on the athletic field or playing floor either during or following games.
- He or she must instruct players regarding the philosophy, objectives, policies and standards of conduct set by the school.
- The coach must repeatedly explain the potential values that interscholastic athletics offer for personality and character development of players. These will not come automatically without guidance.

- He (she) shall distinguish between emphasis on competition and overemphasis on winning. Learning to do one's best is a worthwhile educational goal, but an obsession on winning which causes loss of sight of the educational and recreational values of competition is detrimental to the interscholastic program.
- The coach shall view and cause others to view games in their proper perspective. Although he (she) must stimulate a desire to win, teaching players the enjoyment and values of competing regardless of whether the game is won or lost is a must.
- Standards of sportsmanship and training standards must be developed. Sportsmanship standards contained in game rules and the provisions of the By-Laws for Interscholastics, Sections 11.1 and 11.2 should be carefully explained to players. (See MSHSAA Handbook.) The reasons for these standards must be carefully explained.
- He or she shall know the playing rules and teach players to play within the spirit and intent of them.
- The coach shall enforce the standards of sportsmanship and conduct. Substitution should be made for any player who shows any sign of a display of temper, disgust, etc. A player who is assessed a penalty by a game official for unsportsmanlike conduct should be removed from that game and the player should not be permitted to play in the next succeeding game if the violation is flagrant. Players should understand that intentionally striking a player, etc., will result in their not being permitted to play in the following game. The player must understand that his action casts a reflection on the coach, the entire team, and the school community.
- The standards of eligibility that a student must meet for the privilege of representing his or her school in interscholastic athletics shall be thoroughly reviewed at the beginning of each sport season. A proper understanding of the nonschool competition and award standards is of particular importance (See MSHSAA Handbook, Article VIII, Section 5).

Pep Club
The pep club sponsor shall assume the responsibility of carefully explaining the school's philosophy, objectives, and policies to the cheerleaders and members of the pep club. Other responsibilities which should be assumed include:
- To carefully inform cheerleaders of their responsibility and the standards they must meet. (See *MSHSAA Cheerleaders Guide.*)
- Establish standards of sportsmanship and conduct for members of the pep club. They must be taught to treat visiting students as guests and to extend proper courtesies to them.
- Any act of misbehavior or unsportsmanlike conduct on the part of

students noted by the pep club sponsor should be reported to the high school principal.

The pep club sponsor is urged to review the MSHSAA manual, *Recommended Aids To Sponsors To Improve The Contributions of The Pep Club To The Educational Values of Interscholastics,* which is available from the MSHSAA Office free-of-charge.

Importance of School Effort

The proper planning and administration of the school's interscholastic program cannot be overemphasized. It must be a "team" effort with the high school administrator as the "captain" of the team. Through the administrator's leadership, he or she must "call the plays and see that they are properly executed." The educational and recreational values of interscholastic competition will be improved when this is done.

Procedures And Policies To Be Applied

Sections 11.1 and 11.2 of the By-Laws for Interscholastics provide that each school is responsible for the conduct of its teams, coaches, students, and fans at games both at home and away. (A fan is considered a nonschool student or follower of the school team.) These by-laws further make it clear that the Board of Control has the responsibility to take action when the school does not, or cannot, adequately control the conduct of its players, coaches, and students or fans. The game rules for each sport contain the standards of sportsmanship to be enforced by athletic game officials.

After reviewing recommendations of the Basketball Advisory Committee regarding procedures to be applied when a special report of unsportsmanlike conduct is received by a school, the Board of Control at its June 26, 1972 meeting adopted the following policies to guide member schools and the MSHSAA office in coping with acts of unsportsmanlike conduct.

Procedures For Better Reporting

- Officials shall be required to file a special report with the high school principal no later than 48 hours after penalties have been assessed for unsportsmanlike conduct or any misconduct observed before, during, or following an athletic game. Action shall be taken against officials who fail to file a report.
- Incidents noted by representatives of either of the participating schools, but not observed by the officials, shall be reported to the MSHSAA Office by a school administrator, including action taken if it involves any of that school's players, coaches, students, or fans.
- MSHSAA tournament committees and meet managers shall be required to file reports immediately by telephone followed by a letter regarding any acts of unsportsmanlike conduct.

Action To Be Taken By Schools Upon Receipt Of A Report

- Upon receipt of a special report for unsportsmanlike conduct, the school shall inform the MSHSAA Office in writing of the action being taken to correct or resolve the matter within five days after receipt of the report. exceptions are made for such inadvertent actions a failure to report to the scorer when substituting, wearing a wrong number and other technical infractions not involving flagrant conduct.
- Action regarding unsportsmanlike conduct of a player shall be appropriate to the offense. A player guilty of profane or vulgar language, who deliberately strikes an opposing player or who uses abusive language toward officials, etc., shall be removed from the game by his or her coach and shall not be permitted to participate in the next succeeding game.
- A report of the unsportsmanlike conduct of a coach shall result in action commensurate with the act committed. It may range from a reprimand by the high school administration to conditions set by the board of education that he or she must meet.
- Action regarding the misconduct of a fan shall range from a warning to be required to appear before the board of education to show reason why he or she should not be prohibited from attending future games. Violent acts shall result in charges being brought against the individual or information being provided the prosecuting attorney, who may bring charges under Missouri law without identifying the source of his information.
- Action regarding all other acts of poor sportsmanship shall appropriate to the offense committed.

Authority Delegated Executive Secretary

The Board of Control has delegated to and instructed the MSHSAA Executive Secretary to assume the following authority:

- He shall issue a warning to a school when action taken by it in response to the receipt of a special report of unsportsmanlike conduct or misconduct is not considered satisfactory. Likewise, he shall issue a warning to a school which fails to inform the MSHSAA Office within ten days following the date of a special report received of action taken in regard to it. The warning will be dissolved as of the date the MSHSAA Office receives a reply unless the action taken is not considered satisfactory.

- If a school receives a report during the same sport season after receiving a warning, the high school administrator and the offender shall be required to appear before the Executive Secretary within five days following receipt of the report to show reason why the matter shall not be referred to the Board of Control for consideration under Section 11.1 of the By-Laws for Interscholastics.

- A special report received after a hearing before the Executive Secretary shall automatically be referred to the Board of Control for consideration.
- These guidelines shall not be interpreted to limit the action of the Executive Secretary in any case in which in his opinion immediate or additional action is necessary.
- A school shall have the right to appeal any action taken by the Executive Secretary to the Board of Control.

It is strongly recommended that all coaches and students be thoroughly informed of these policies adopted by the Board of Control and that it be carefully explained to them that the primary purpose of these policies is to improve the educational and recreational values which interscholastic athletic games can have for our high school youth. If these values are lost, interscholastic competition can no longer be justified in the school program!

APPENDIX B

A NOTE TO CONTEST ADMINISTRATORS

In theory, school administrators, athletic directors, coaches, athletes and officials have the same objectives in mind with regard to any officiating program. As in any field, the caliber of men and women who are attracted to the work bears a relationship to the working conditions that prevail. In other words, if you want good officials, treat them right!

The National Federation of State High School Associations says it better than I could have:

Most officials continue in the work because it is an avocation which provides opportunity to maintain contact with the game and with those who administer the contests. If responsible and highly respected men are to be kept in the field, they should be accorded the cordial and businesslike treatment they expect in the professions and in other vocation. They are requested to render decisions in rather technical matters and in an atmosphere charged with prejudice and emotion. No effort should be spared in providing conditions which will be conducive to efficiency and pleasant associations. Each contest administrator owes this to the Official who is his guest and to the school which must depend on the work being of such a nature as to attract men who are in the habit of being treated with respect.

In practical terms, officials have a right to expect that host management will be mindful of certain considerations:

- An official never has a "home game." He should therefore be made to feel welcome by being placed in adequate dressing facilities and escorted to and from the dressing area to the playing area.
- Adequate security should be on hand and visible.
- Police and security personnel should be instructed to take whatever steps necessary to prosecute any violent behavior quickly and decisively.
- Officials should be paid prior to the game and not asked to fill out forms or otherwise be detained after the contest is completed.
- The benefits of good sportsmanship should be continually reinforced through education of not only student athletes, but coaching personnel and other faculty.
- Spectators should not be permitted to mill around near the playing surface or otherwise interfere with the duties of officials.
- Great care should be taken, for the protection of all concerned, to see that the playing area complies fully with the rules and that all equipment meets the prescribed safety standards. Should any of these items be found deficient by the officials, remember that it is their duty to make required corrections before play is commenced or resumed.

APPENDIX C
THE BASEBALL UMPIRE: A VIEW FROM 1900

The whole of North America is intensely interested, and with good reason, in baseball, a game I should like to introduce into France. It is played all over the United States by two teams of nine men each, with an unlimited number of substitutes, the various positions in the field being allotted strictly in accordance with capacity and long experience. The players' object, after the ball is in play, is to get first to the bases at the four angles of a diamond marked out in a very large enclosure. On each side the principal positions are held by specialists; on one, the pitcher and the catcher, and, on the other, the batter. From the center of the diamond, the pitcher hurls the ball at his comrade the catcher, who stands just behind the corner of the diamond, or home plate, padded from head to foot and wears a special kind of glove and a strong mask. His business is to catch the ball, very much as a circus athlete stops a cannon ball. Between the pitcher and the catcher is the batter, who stands firmly, waits for the ball and does his best to hit it as far as possible with a masterly stroke of his bat. If he succeeds, as he often does, he takes advantage of the few moments in which the ball is flying through space to run to the first base, and then the second and third if he has time; but one of his far-distant opponents catches the ball and throws it to one of the men at the base, who can thus forestall the batter, and it remains to be seen whether the batter will be the first to reach the base. A whole city-full of people, sometimes as many as 40,000 spectators, in great cities like Pittsburgh or Chicago, turns out to see one of these matches, cheer the players and give way to enthusiasm or exasperation. The runner, in his efforts to beat the speed of the ball, generally throws himself at full length on the ground and just touches the base with his finger or foot, or misses it by an inch, and then there is a terrific out-burst of excitement, shouting, stamping and gesticulating among the spectators, who cannot always tell whether the runner is successful or not. In the big matches, when two famous teams are playing, and when one city is pitted against another, Brooklyn against St. Louis, for instance; when two champion clubs two baseball "giants" or "pheno-menons" stand face to face in front of their anxious supporters, the crowd cannot contain itself. But, behind the catcher, a young man, quite different from the rest, stands motionless. He wears a long coat, a breastplate and a mask. He watches the game, and when the dis-puting over a run is at its height and the crowd threatens to invade the ground, he intervenes. A sign from him stops the shouting and res-tores quiet. He decides who has won and who has lost.

Who is this mysterious personage and extraordinary authority? He is the umpire. He is selected from among the college students, or, on great occasions, among the most celebrated professionals and best judges of the game. He is brought all the way from Boston or Chi-cago, and he is paid like a man who has a reputation to keep up. I have more than once used him as an example, to the great delight of my hearers. I have demonstrated that if it is possible to stop the rush of the baseball players (who must not dispute the umpire, even if he is wrong) and restrains crowds electrified by the excitement of the game, it is much less difficult to stop two equally civilized nations whose governments are preparing to mobilize them. It is a question of education in governmental responsibility, a question of mutual inter-est properly understood, and also of discipline. After I had demon-strated this proposition all over the United States, an objection was raised to the effect that the umpire is sometimes rather badly treated by the crowd. "Kill the umpire!" was heard not very long ago. In Amer-ica, no doubt, as in other countries, a man who has lost his case does not deny himself the pleasure of saying what he thinks about the judge, but it is none the less true that the whole organization of baseball, which is no less popular than the barbarous bull-fighting in Spain and is infinitely more general, is based on absolute and undisputed obedience to the umpire. The same is true of many other games, notably football. It is an excellent form of physical and moral training.

—From *America and Her Problems*
   by D'Estournelles de Constant

INDEX

N

Negligence, legal	20, 21-22, 32-39
New Jersey State Interscholastic Athletic Association	53
Newspapers, interviews with	17, 102, 103-104
NOCSAE	47, 69, 70
Nose, protective device for	57
Nosebleeds (wrestling)	99-100

O

Objective of officiating	14, 16
Officials' associations, suits against	125-128
Officiating, professional and ethical approach	17
Out of bounds, coverage of (football)	74

P

Partiality, appearance of	16, 17-18
Pennsylvania Interscholastic Athletic Association	60
Photographers' line (soccer)	82
Physicians at wrestling matches	93, 99
Pitcher, undershirt of	47
Players, supervision of between quarters (football)	78
Police	108, 114-122
Prevention of injuries (wrestling), see Wrestling, injuries	
Proximate cause	21, 36, 37
Pylons (football)	13-14, 68

R

Rain, effect of	50
Reasonable person standard in law	20
Reasonably prudent official	20
Red card (soccer)	85
Relationship, officials with school personnel	16
Reports of officials	105-110
Respondeat superior	22, 24, 25
Robert's Rules of Order	130-131
Rule enforcement, intelligent	14, 15

S

Safety of players	25-26, 45, 56, 57-58, 68, 85, 89-90
School boards	25, 34